FRAY
JUNIPERO
SERRA

Mark Brunelle

dp

Published by Dobronte Publications
P.O. Box 4521 • Carmel-By-The-Sea, Ca. 93921

– to Father Serra

Here is an intimate look at Father Junipero Serra: the priest, the person, and the spirit — this wonderful, humble, champion of humanity. During his fourteen years in California, he did much more than merely establish nine Franciscan Missions. He stood as a guardian and protector of the native Indians, as well as an inspiration to the Spaniards — who came to claim the New World California as their own. By his constant mediation and example he moved men and mountains. Ever humble, ever in the service of the Lord, he referred to himself simply as: Fray Junipero Serra — This most unworthy priest.

— *Suggested reading by the*
SERRA BICENTENNIAL COMMISSION
Newsletter. Issue 7. September 1984.
Msgr. Francis J. Weber, Executive Secretary.

FRAY
JUNIPERO
SERRA

Mark Brunelle

Illustrated by Kelly Steele and Jeffrey Helwig
DOBRONTE PUBLICATIONS MCMLXXXIV

Spanish Missions
founded in California by
Father Junipero Serra

San Diego de Alcalá	July 16, 1769
San Carlos Borromeo de Carmelo	June 3, 1770
San Antonio de Padua	July 14, 1771
San Gabriel Arcángel	September 8, 1771
San Luis Obispo de Tolosa	September 1, 1772
San Francisco de Asís	June 29, 1776
San Juan Capistrano	November 1, 1776
Santa Clara de Asís	January 12, 1777
San Buenaventura	March 31, 1782

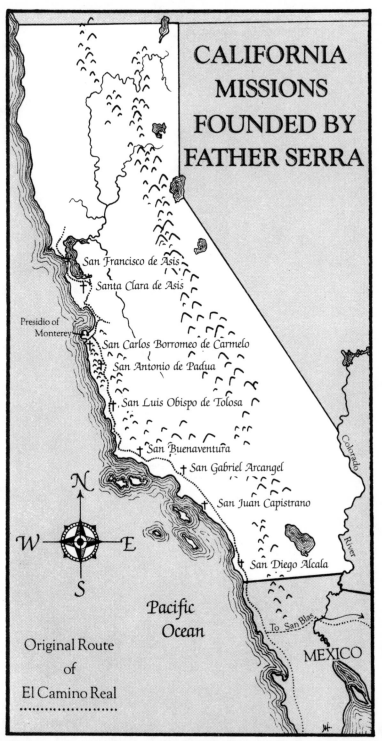

CALIFORNIA
MISSIONS
FOUNDED BY
FATHER SERRA

San Francisco de Asis

Santa Clara de Asis

Presidio of
Monterey

San Carlos Borromeo de Carmelo

San Antonio de Padua

San Luis Obispo de Tolosa

San Buenaventura

San Gabriel Arcangel

San Juan Capistrano

San Diego Alcala

Colorado

River

N

W — E

S

Pacific
Ocean

To San Blas

MEXICO

Original Route
of
El Camino Real
....

INTRODUCTION

During the 15th and 16th centuries, Spain colonized most of the New World. In 1542, San Diego was discovered and charted by the Portuguese navigator, Juan Rodríguez Cabrillo, who was employed by the Spanish government.

On November 11th of that year Cabrillo sighted Monterey Bay. He carefully charted its location, but a storm prevented a landing party from being sent ashore. Sixty years later, Sebastián Vizcaíno used Cabrillo's maps to locate Monterey Bay. The plans to build settlements were abandoned and there was no new Spanish exploration in upper California until Father Junípero Serra came north to found the Mission San Diego, in 1769, with the expedition that was led by Gaspár de Portolá.

Father Serra was born on November 24, 1713, in Petra, Mallorca, and he died on August 28, 1784, at the Mission San Carlos in Carmel, California. He was already a noted teacher and lecturer when he left his homeland in Spain, at the age of thirty-five, to pursue his boyhood dream of working with the Indian people in the New World. Serra served as a priest in Mexico for nineteen years before he set out for the unexplored region to the north. He was fifty-six years old and his health was failing when he founded his first mission at San Fernando de Velicata, in Baja California. By the time his work was finished, he had established a total of nine Spanish missions in what is now the state of California.

Although the little priest was only 5' 2" tall and weighed barely 110 pounds, he was a man of boundless energy and determination. He traveled by ship, mule, and on foot, covering more than 24,000 miles. His work took him across more territory than the combined journeys of Christopher Columbus and Marco Polo. Any attempt to chart his exact, day-to-day movements would have defeated my purpose in this project. While studying the early Spanish mission period of California history, I discovered that I was much more captivated and inspired by the life and work of

Father Junípero Serra than I was by a long list of dates and places. I examined instead the political, social, and economic realities of the time and I endeavored to gain new perspectives and insights into the life of a unique man. The letters that were written by his friends and former students, Fathers Palóu and Crespi, were very supportive of Father Serra and his work. But carrying my study one important step further, I also carefully examined what was written by those who were not as cooperative with the Father Presidente and his efforts. I was very pleased, but in no way surprised, to discover that they were as amazed by the indomitable spirit of Father Junípero Serra as I was.

Many people come to Mission San Carlos in Carmel, California, looking for an epitaph for Father Serra. None is needed, for Christopher Wren's epitaph applies: *Si Monumentum Requiris, Circumspice* . . . "If you seek a monument, look about you."

San Carlos Borromeo de Carmelo

CHAPTER I

HE desert country between San Fernando de Velicata in Baja California and San Diego in upper California stretched out for hundreds of miles. The vegetation was scarce, the terrain scattered with rocks, and fresh drinking-water difficult to locate. The expedition of eighty men, led by Gaspár de Portolá, encountered these harsh conditions when they set out to found the first mission in the new land and claim the territory north of Mexico for the King of Spain.

The late afternoon sun was beating down relentlessly. Intense heat radiated from the hot sand and occasionally a jackrabbit was driven from the shelter of the scrub growth that lined the old animal migration trail that the expedition was following. As they stumbled along, the sun's blinding brightness flashed on the tips of their lances. The air was filled with the dust kicked up by the hooves of heavily-laden pack mules.

Earlier, an old man had been limping along in the middle of the group of Christian Indians, muleteers, and soldiers. Now he was steadily falling back. The old man, clad in the gray robe and white-cord belt of the Franciscan Order, was Father Junípero Serra. A twelve-inch cross hung at his side swaying with each step he took. His face was covered with dust, perspiration, and an expression of intense pain as he dragged his swollen leg behind him. He had been bitten by a mosquito soon after he arrived at Vera Cruz. The bite became infected and the condition was to worsen throughout the remainder of his life.

A soldier at the rear of the troop looked back and saw that Father Serra was unable to keep up. When the padre was some thirty yards behind, the soldier decided to help the old man. He stopped and waited for Father Serra to catch up, then put his arm around the shorter man's waist and smiled. "Lean on me, Padre."

Father Serra put his arm around the soldier and returned a smile of weariness. "Thank you."

1

The two men continued to walk slowly. "Did you turn your ankle, Padre?"

"No, my son. I have had this affliction since I came to the New World."

The soldier looked concerned. "Are you sure that you can complete this journey?"

Father Serra stared straight ahead and walked with determination. "The Lord will see that I make it."

The soldier shook his head in disbelief. He could see the main body of the expedition nearing the top of a distant hill where Captain Portolá waited for the group to catch up with him. When Portolá looked back and saw that the soldier and Father Serra were at least two hundred yards behind, he ordered the troop to keep marching, then he snapped the reins and galloped back toward the stragglers. The prancing steed glided down the hillside as if it had wings. Its tail and mane waved in the wind. The soldier heard the beating hooves and looked to see Portolá riding toward them. "Here comes the Captain," he said, "and it looks like he's angry."

Stopping the horse in front of them, Portolá removed his hat and wiped the perspiration from his face with his dusty sleeve. "If you can't keep up, Padre," he stated, "I wish you'd turn back right now. It's only a few days' ride back to Velicata."

Father Serra straightened up and stood erect with the soldier's assistance. "I'll never turn back," he said with conviction.

Portolá sighed. "You have founded your mission, Padre."

"Mission San Fernando is in lower California. My job is hardly complete."

Portolá jammed his hat back on his head. "If your condition isn't better soon, I shall have you carried back to Velicata!" he said angrily, then slapped his horse on the flank and galloped away.

The soldier and Father Serra watched as the captain disappeared over the top of the hill. "We'd better keep going, Padre," the man said, "or we won't catch up until morning."

Father Serra wiped his face with a cloth and then replaced it in his sleeve. "I am ready."

The soldier put his arm around the padre and they plodded along once again. Although the sun had begun to drop in the sky, the heat grew even more intense. Twilight came rapidly, then nightfall. It was dark by the time they reached the top of the distant hill. The soldier pointed to the base of the next hill where he could see the light of many small cooking fires. "The camp is only about a mile away," he said.

"Let's keep going," the padre urged.

The two men struggled through the darkness until they came to the edge of the camp. Sentries were marching back and forth with muskets on their shoulders. When a twig cracked, their weapons snapped into position and one called out, "Who goes there?"

"Corporal José Ortega," the soldier answered. "And Father Junípero Serra."

The sentries relaxed and watched Ortega and Father Serra emerge from the brush. In the reflected light of the campfire, they appeared dirty, perspiration-streaked, and exhausted. Corporal Ortega led Father Serra through the middle of the camp until he found a small, unoccupied fire. He took a blanket from a pack that was sitting against a large rock, made a pallet for Father Serra, then helped the old man ease himself to the ground. "You stay here and rest, Padre, and I'll find both of us something to eat."

Father Serra reached down and began to remove his sandals. "Take care of yourself first, my son."

As Ortega disappeared, Serra pulled his robe up to his knees to examine his swollen legs. They were worse then yesterday; two painful falls on the rocks in the darkness had not helped. They were covered with ulcers and brush cuts. Hearing heavy footsteps, he quickly pulled his robe down over his feet. When he looked up, Captain Portola was before him and the light from the small fire was gleaming in his dark eyes. "I have seen what you are trying to hide, Father," he said, "and now I am certain that you cannot make this journey." He paused in thought. "Therefore, I must insist that you go back to Velicata just as soon as you are able to travel."

Father Serra rose to his feet, showing no signs of pain. "I have put my trust in God, who has permitted me to travel this far. If it is His will that I should die on the way, then bury me in the road and I will be content to remain forever in the company of the gentiles."

A look of frustration appeared on Portolá's face. "I shall have a stretcher made and you will be carried by the Indians."

"I won't hear of it," Father Serra said decisively. "The burden could kill them!"

"My dear Padre," he said with exasperation in his voice, "wouldn't it be better to lose just a few Indians than to have all of us slowed down in the desert and perish for the lack of water?"

"I shall pray for our deliverance."

"It is my responsibility to see that this expedition reaches its destination," Portolá said angrily. "I will not have our mission threatened by a stubborn, old fool such as yourself!"

Father Serra sat down on the blanket and folded his arms across his knees. "I fully understand your responsibilities and I also understand my own." He turned his head toward approaching footsteps.

Corporal Ortega appeared with a plate of food in each hand; his smile disappeared as he sensed the tension between the two men. He put the plates down beside the fire and stood at attention before Portolá.

"Who commanded you attend the sick?" the officer demanded.

"The Master whom he serves," Ortega said as he pointed to Father Serra.

3

Portolá put both hands behind his back and rocked forward on his feet. "I cannot fight him and his Master."

The corporal was still standing at attention. "Would you like me to leave, Captain?"

"You stay here with the padre. If he cannot travel by morning, make a stretcher and find two of the strongest Indians to carry it," he said. "I can't spare any soldiers. We could be attacked."

Father Serra looked up at the captain. "I will not be carried by anyone."

"Then you will ride a mule," Portolá insisted.

"It is much too painful to have my leg jarred by the quick gait of a nervous animal. It's better if I just walk."

Captain Portolá removed his hat and slapped it across his left hand. "Come to your senses, man. Lives are at stake here."

Corporal Ortega stepped forward between the two angry men. Portolá growled. "You have an idea, Corporal?"

Ortega stroked at the side of his head. "I might have a solution."

"Let's hear it," Portolá said, sighing in resignation. "I'm all out of ideas."

"Do you know Juan Antonio Coronel?"

"Yes. He's the muleteer."

Ortega spoke nervously. "He must have some sort of remedy."

Portolá put his hat back on. "I doubt if it will do any good but at this point I'd try anything."

Ortega looked up at the captain. "Then shall I fetch my friend?"

"At once!"

As the corporal marched toward the area where all of the animals were tethered, Father Serra looked up at the captain again. His voice was bemused as he said, "To be attended to by a muleteer . . . it must be the will of God."

Portolá laughed. "I wouldn't let a veterinarian take a sliver out of my thumb."

"I have been praying for several days," Father Serra insisted. "This must be the will of God."

"You haven't slept in three days, Padre. Even if your foot were as good as new, you couldn't keep up with us."

"Then I must pray harder," Father Serra said as the corporal appeared with Juan Antonio Coronel. The muleteer was laden with mixing bowls and pouches full of herbs.

Ortega stood at attention and held his breath. "This is Juan Antonio, Captain."

Father Serra pulled his robe up to his knees. "My son," he said, "do you have some remedy to cure me?"

The muleteer bent down on one knee and examined Father Serra's legs. He sucked in his breath sharply and there was concern in his voice when he said, "Padre, I am not a physician. I cure only beasts."

4

"Then assume than I am a beast and I am afflicted by a saddle gall."

"I beg your indulgence, Padre, but . . . "

"Treat me as if I were one of your animals," Father Serra insisted as he reached out and held firmly onto Juan Antonio's shoulder.

Juan smiled. "To please you Padre, I shall do as you request. And when I am finished I shall pray that the grace of God will make you well."

Father Serra moved closer to the fire so the light would reveal his affliction and pulled up his robe again. Captain Portolá turned and walked rapidly away when he saw the sores and ulcers that covered the old man's lower extremities.

Juan Antonio placed the bowls on the ground next to Father Serra. He pounded some tallow between two rocks and stirred the concoction as he added herbs from several of the leather pouches. Juan Antonio heated the mixture over the fire, then took a handful and prepared to apply it to Father Serra's sores. "Forgive me, Padre. I must cause you more pain."

Father Serra clasped his hands around the large cross that hung at his side. "Go ahead, my son."

Juan Antonio began to apply a liberal amount of the hot, sticky substance to the Padre's legs. "You will have to rest or the remedy will not be able to do its work."

"But we are leaving early in the morning and I have to make so many . . . ," Father Serra winced as Juan Antonio's remedy burned in the open sores. Ortega watched the fingers of the little priest turn white as they tightly gripped the cross. Long moments later, Juan Antonio finished. He wiped his hands on a cloth and said, "You must do as I ask, Padre, and rest."

Father Serra pushed his robe down over his legs, went back to his blanket and sat down. "But you don't understand."

The muleteer picked up his bowls and pouches of herbs. "When a mule is stubborn, I lash his feet together so that he is hobbled. I hope that I don't have to do this to you, my friend."

Ortega began to laugh. "I shall see that he rests, Juan."

"I shall see you again in the morning, Padre," Juan Antonio said as he walked away.

"Thank you, my son," Father Serra answered, blessing the man with the sign of the cross.

Corporal Ortega covered Father Serra with his own blanket, put some more wood on the small fire, and, as he sat down beside the glowing embers, pulled his hat down over his eyes.

Father Serra held his crucifix to his breast with both hands and looked up at the star-filled sky. "What is your full name?" he asked the corporal.

"José Francisco Ortega."

"Do you have a family?"

"A wife and a son, Padre."

"I will pray for our success," he said, "so you can send for them soon."

5

Corporal Ortega pushed his hat back and looked over at Father Serra. "When a man is away from his family, there can be problems. Some of the soldiers have been talking about what they'd do if they were to come across an Indian woman."

"I will pray for a miracle then."

"I understand why you're so determined, Padre. Someone must look after the Indians."

Father Serra reached down and touched his legs lightly. "The remedy seems to be working. I cannot feel them any longer."

Corporal Ortega pulled his hat down over his eyes. "Go to sleep, Padre. We have many miles to travel in the morning."

Father Serra prayed quietly as he looked up at the night sky. Ortega leaned back against a rock; he was asleep within seconds.

When dawn came, the corporal was still asleep with his hat over his face. He woke as he heard someone approaching. A quick glance confirmed the fact that Father Serra wasn't in his bed. Ortega jumped up and stood at attention as Captain Portolá appeared. "Good morning, Captain!" he said as he remained erect.

The captain had an Army uniform jacket across his arm. "At ease, Sergeant!" he answered.

Ortega looked confused. "Sergeant?"

The captain tossed his jacket to Ortega. "See if this fits."

Ortega caught the jacket in the air and examined the stripes that were stitched onto the sleeves. "Yes, sir!"

Portolá smiled. "Are you tired of walking yet?"

Ortega removed his own coat, slipped into the one that Portolá had given him and buttoned up the jacket. "A soldier does his duty, Captain."

"Good," the officer said. "From now on you'll be riding point until we get to San Diego. Go pick out a good mount."

The sergeant looked over at Father Serra's empty bed. "Where's the Padre, sir?"

The captain shook his head in disbelief. "He's saying Mass."

Ortega looked surprised. "But he could barely stand last night."

Portolá shrugged, then pointed. "Go see for yourself."

Ortega saluted the captain and turned and walked across the camp. He soon heard the voices of the men as they sang a hymn, then he stopped in his tracks; Father Serra was moving around briskly, without any signs of pain. Juan Antonio Coronel was standing in the back row as Ortega walked up behind him and whispered, "I can't believe it."

Juan Antonio turned and faced Ortega. "Last night I thought he would be crippled for life . . . that he was a dead man."

Ortega sighed. "Could you find young José Maria and have him look out for the Padre?" he asked. "I'll be riding point until we get to San Diego."

"The young Indian boy?"

"Yes," Ortega said quietly. "He worships the Padre."

"Sure."

"I have to pick out a mount this morning."

Coronel smiled. "Take the buckskin. He's strong."

"Thanks," Ortega said, and walked away.

Juan Antonio nodded his head and turned to face the altar. The soldiers had begun to line up for Communion. In the east, the sun broke away from a range of hills and its golden rays brought a new day to the camp as the little Franciscan priest went about his work with a smiling face.

For the rest of his life, Juan Antonio Coronel was to remember Father Serra as he appeared that morning. The sun's rays had highlighted his face and his crucifix glowed as if it were illuminated from within. As the priest raised his arms in benediction, his elongated shadow fell across the makeshift altar and touched all who were near him.

"Surely," Juan Antonio thought," this is a man of God."

CHAPTER II

N the heat of the blazing sun, the expedition continued northward. Day after day the troop traveled quickly, prodded on by Captain Portolá. Each soldier had a determined look on his dirty, bearded face. In one area, where signs of hostile Indians had been spotted, the dust from their march rose in a thick, beige cloud that could be seen for miles.

Nervous glances were exchanged by the soldiers, indicating that these professionals were aware of the possible dangers surrounding them; each canyon could hide an ambush, each mountain pass was an invitation for danger.

At night, the picket lines were drawn closer together, the fires built higher. Guards on duty did not have to be told to keep a sharp lookout. High in the powder-blue Mexican sky, the vultures circled patiently.

Then, gradually, the land began to change from a harsh desert to a semi-arid, more hospitable climate. Once, as they crested a hill, José Maria glanced toward the west and sucked in his breath in alarm as he saw a solid gray bank of clouds beyond the far ridge of hills.

"A storm, Padre. Look!" he said, twisting around on his mule and pointing.

"No, my son," Serra said with a smile, "that's a fog bank. Beyond those hills must lie the ocean."

"How far have we come now?"

"Captain Portolá told me last night that he estimated we have traveled almost 600 miles."

"How much farther do we have to go?" It was a question the boy asked every day and it was usually answered with a shrug.

Today, however, the priest looked thoughtfully toward the fog bank and ahead toward the westward sloping hills. "I think . . . perhaps, God willing, only two or three more days."

In the distance, near the crest of the hill, Serra could see the lone figure of Sergeant José Ortega riding scout about five miles in front of the expedition. As he watched, the horseman rode out of sight.

Out there, Ortega's attention was focused on the hillsides. All day yesterday there had been signs of Indians, on foot of course, since this expedition was bringing the first horses into California. He had given his information to Captain Portolá who had looked grim, then told him not to speak of it to the other soldiers.

The sergeant was suddenly startled as a flight of wild pigeons took to the air with a great beating of wings. There were thousands of birds and the air turned black with them. Laughing at his own nervousness, Ortega followed them with his eyes and then saw what they had all been praying for!

Down below, in the distance, were the blue waters of the Pacific. Two ships were at anchor and some Spanish soldiers were camped near the edge of a sandy beach. Ortega whipped off his hat and waved it, yelling in excitement, but they were too far away to hear. He turned his horse around and galloped back to tell Captain Portolá of his discovery. Ortega drew his pistol from its holster and, when he finally had the expedition in sight, he fired a shot.

Captain Portolá, hearing the shot, stopped the caravan and ordered the soldiers to stand ready with their muskets. Father Serra rode up to the captain and asked, "What is it?"

"I heard a pistol shot," Portolá answered, looking at him.

"Sergeant Ortega?"

"It must be. It came from a great distance."

Father Serra made the sign of the cross and prayed. The captain and the padre sat there and waited, listening as the sound of the beating hooves drew closer. Sergeant Ortega finally came riding in through a grove of scrub oaks, galloping at full speed, his hat bouncing up and down on his back.

"San Diego is over the next hill!" he yelled.

A smile appeared on Portolá's face and a loud cheer went up from the eighty-man expedition as they realized that they were near the end of their long journey. Ortega stopped his horse abruptly in front of the captain. He looked excited but serious as he saluted the officer. "I think we should keep a sharp lookout. There are many Indians nearby."

Portolá nodded, then asked the question foremost in all of their minds. "Did any of the ships make it?"

"Yes, sir."

A sigh of relief passed over the captain's lips. "We'll have plenty of supplies."

Father Serra nudged his mule to the sergeant's side. "How many Indians are there?" he asked.

"There must be ten or fifteen thousand, scattered all over these hills."

Portolá turned to his men. "Keep your eyes open!" he commanded.

"I could see a lot of graves from the top of the hill," Ortega said, frowning. "There's no way of knowing if death was caused by sickness or attack from some hostiles."

Portolá raised his arm into the air. "March!" he commanded.

Sergeant Ortega rode out ahead of the expedition again. He waited on the top of the hill that overlooked the two ships. This time a sentry saw Ortega sitting astride his horse. Quickly he told Lieutenant Don Fernando Rivera, who called together a small contingent of soldiers and proceeded toward the hilltop.

Ortega climbed down from his horse and waited for them. He could see Portolá leading the expedition up to the top of the rise from the other side. The captain got there first, followed by Father Serra and the Indian boy.

Father Serra made the sign of the cross when he saw the encampment below. He climbed down from the mule and handed the reins to young Jose María. "I knew that we'd make it . . . by the grace of God."

"There were supposed to be three ships," Portolá said.

"The other one may show up yet," Father Serra answered as he made the sign of the cross again.

The small contingent of soldiers arrived with Lieutenant Rivera. They were out of breath and they sat down as soon as they reached the top of the hill. The officer spoke first. "There is much sickness in our camp."

"We will stay far away from you then, Don Fernando," Portolá said.

"We have buried over thirty sailors."

"What about your soldiers, Lieutenant Rivera?"

"Three are dead and many are dying."

"We will be leaving to find Monterey in about a week."

"All of you, Captain?"

"Most of us," he said. "I can't leave my men here to die of this sickness."

Rivera sighed. "The Indians here have been threatening us with attack and we were relieved to see your numbers."

"Have they caused you any trouble?"

"No, Captain. But it's only a matter of time, for they watch from the hills as we bury our dead."

"What have you done to offend them?"

"Nothing, Captain. But I did hear that a couple of my men went out and found some female company."

Captain Portolá glared at Rivera. "You control your men or they'll face a firing squad!"

"Yes, sir!"

"There are too many Indians in these hills for a small squad like ours to handle."

"Is that all, Captain?"

Father Serra stepped up close to Captain Portolá. "May I ask the Lieutenant a question?"

"By all means, Padre."

"How are Father Gomez and my dear friend, Father Juan Crespí?"

Rivera pointed down the hillside. "A bit overworked, Padre. You can see the rows of crosses from here . . . but other than that, they're both fine."

The rest of the men in Portolá's expedition finally reached the top of the hill. They let out a cheer as they gazed at the ocean below. As Father Serra walked down to Rivera's camp, he stopped suddenly and an expression of pleasure illuminated his face. There, growing out of the rocks, was a small bush. A tiny flower glowed with bright, living color; it was the small, pink blossom of a wild rose, a Rose of Castile!

The first week passed quickly. On the morning of the eighth day, Father Serra went up to the top of the hill and remained there as the *San Antonio* set sail with the morning tide. Captain Portolá, accompanied by his troops, watched with Father Serra. When the wind billowed out the sails, the vessel began to make its way out into the open water. "The *San Antonio* will return with more supplies," Captain Portolá said to the padre, "and my men and I will return after we have located Monterey."

Father Serra blessed the members of the expedition. "May God go with you, Captain."

José Maria appeared just as Captain Portolá gave the command to start the long, 400-mile march to Monterey. Father Serra and his young friend stood and watched until the rear guard had passed them. Then they walked down the hillside together.

There was work to be done; they had a mission to build.

San Diego Alcála

CHAPTER III

HE Mission San Diego was founded, early in the morning, on July 16, 1769. Father Serra sprinkled some holy water onto a large wooden cross that was lying on the ground. After concluding his short prayer, he stepped aside and the timber was raised by several soldiers and Christian Indians. Everyone cheered as the heavy cross dropped into the deep hole with a resounding thud.

A soldier carried the Spanish flag on a pole and stuck it into the ground beside the raised cross. Sergeant Ortega took a handful of dirt, held it high over his head, and yelled with a bellowing voice, "I claim this land for Charles III, the King of Spain!"

The soldiers discharged their muskets, the bell was rung, and the cannon on the *San Carlos* were discharged. The soldiers in attendance cheered with raised hands. The celebration that followed was a short one since the supplies were low and the usual feast for such a special occasion could not be prepared.

Work on the mission buildings, and the stockade, began the next day. Father Serra and Sergeant Ortega supervised in the construction of several small, wooden sheds and the short stockade walls. Some of the men drove sharpened stakes into the sandy soil, while others thatched roofs to cap the tops of the crude structures. The cook-shack was the only building constructed of adobe, to make it safe from fire.

Indians watched the activity from the distant hills. Most were clad in breech cloths but some were stark naked. Their faces were painted, their skin was darkly tanned, and they carried spears and bows and arrows.

Some of the soldiers were still dying from scurvy. The funerals were conducted under the cover of darkness so the Indians wouldn't be sure of the exact numbers inhabiting the small stockade.

On the morning of August 15th, Father Serra and José Maria were sitting on the top of the hill where Captain Portolá had camped earlier. It was a peaceful morning and the birds were singing while the people

13

worked in the mission compound. José looked over Father Serra's shoulder as the old man read to him from a small prayer book. They were both at ease but their mood changed suddenly as a shot rang out from the small compound below. Father Serra and young José watched, appalled, as waves of Indians swept down the hillside, vaulted the short stockade walls, and entered the mission. A large hospital tent was crowded with soldiers who had been sick for weeks. The feverish men were resting on cots that were made up with dirty sheets. The sickness had drained them of all of their energy and they could only lie there and await their fates.

What the Indians had come for was soon apparent to the soldiers, as the warriors rolled the invalids onto the ground and took the linens from their beds. When the Indians had accomplished their goal, they streaked across the compound and escaped over the short, wooden barrier. Several of them had fallen, mortally wounded, still clutching the sheets that they had taken.

Sergeant Ortega urged his men to fight in the thick of the confusion. The soldiers fired their muskets and reloaded them frantically. The Indians' arrows bounced harmlessly off the soldiers' heavy leather vests and bullhide shields.

Father Serra and José watched the battle from the distance. The old man finally rose to his feet. "You stay here until I send for you," he said to his young friend. "I must go to the chapel and protect the consecrated host."

The boy watched as Father Serra ran down the steep hillside. José was worried about the little priest because he knew of the reputation of the Indians who inhabited the area around San Diego. As the padre entered the compound, the boy paused a moment and then bolted after his friend, thinking the padre might need his protection.

Father Serra entered the chapel and went to the tabernacle to make the sign of the cross. He opened the door of a small safe and removed the golden chalice that contained several consecrated hosts. The old man began to pray in Latin, dropped to his knees, and consumed them.

José Maria finally reached the compound. He ran through the confusion and jumped over the body of a dead Indian. As he reached for the handle of the chapel door, he did not see another warrior, with an arrow cocked, step out from behind a stack of crates and wooden boxes. The bow string twanged as the deadly missile was sent whispering on its way.

José grabbed at his throat as the arrow passed through his neck. As the Indian let out a war cry, José burst through the chapel door and fell at Father Serra's feet. The boy was spitting up blood and he was choking. "Father . . . give me . . . absolution," he pled, reaching up to his friend with both hands.

Father Serra burst into tears as he knelt to cradle the dying boy's head in his lap. "My son!"

José put his arms around Father Serra's waist. "Quickly, Father, for I am dying!"

14

Father Serra's eyes were filled with tears as he rocked the youth in his arms and began a prayer in Latin. Although the battle continued to rage outside, neither was aware of anything but the final absolution. The boy's blood had soaked the priest's robe by the time Father Serra concluded his prayer. A moment of silence ensued, then José Maria looked up and closed his eyes.

"They have killed me," he said softly and died.

When Father Serra emerged from the chapel with José in his arms, his gray robe was covered with bright red blood. Sergeant Ortega looked over at the padre and ran to him immediately, his voice full of concern. "Are you all right?"

Father Serra was filled with great sadness. "I have lost a friend," he said as he fought back the tears. "One whom I loved with all of my heart."

"We have no other casualties."

"We can thank God for that," the padre responded as he stood looking down at the lifeless body of José Maria.

Sergeant Ortega ordered a nearby soldier, "Take the boy to my quarters and prepare his body for burial."

Father Serra handed the dead youth gently to the soldier and then wiped the tears from his face with the sleeve of his garment. "What caused the attack?"

"Captain Portolá's order."

"What?"

Sergeant Ortega looked seriously at the padre. "Before we got here the Indians were trading their women for cloth. But Portolá's order to leave the women alone changed all of that."

"You can't mean that!" Father Serra said in a state of shock. He stared around at the bodies of the dead and wounded Indians. "All of this for a few pieces of dirty linen?"

Ortega studied the little priest. "It looks like you've got your work cut out for you, doesn't it, my friend?" He could see that the moaning, sick soldiers needed help to get back into their small cots so he walked back to the hospital tent.

Father Serra followed the sergeant. "There's a lot more to founding a mission than just raising a cross and constructing some buildings."

"Right you are, Padre. We both have work to do. I must secure this compound and double the guard and hope that Portolá and his soldiers get back before the Indians out there realize how few of us there are left."

"I have confidence in your abilities, my son. I only pray that I am worthy of my own task."

Sergeant Ortega directed the soldiers to build the stockade walls much higher than they had been. As the hammers and axes rang through the day and late into the night, an inventory was taken to count the supplies. Armed guards watched, with their muskets at ready, as a large group of

Indians threatened them from a distance with screams and gestures of defiance.

When mealtime came, the soldiers passed by with their bowls in hand. They were weak from hunger and they were given a small ration of bread and hot soup. None of them could have realized how precarious their situation was to become. They were to suffer for two more months before the winter rains finally came.

Sergeant Ortega sat in his small office late into the night, examining the reports that were piled in front of him on his desk. A small insubstantial fire flickered in the fireplace and several oil lamps made the atmosphere smoky. He turned at a knock on the door. A soldier opened it up from the outside to let Father Serra enter the room. "Sit beside the fire and warm yourself, Padre," Ortega said as he rose to his feet.

With a groan of relief, the little priest sat in the chair and began to rub his hands together near the flames. "How does it look?"

"I don't know how much longer we can hold out," Ortega responded. "I really don't."

"We'll make it by the grace of God."

"You don't understand, Padre. We've been on less than half-rations since Portolá left. Soon, very soon, we'll be on quarter rations. And now the rain! Every day another man becomes ill . . . " He shook his head in frustration.

"But the *San Antonio* sailed back to San Blas to get more supplies."

"Captain Portolá would march us back to Mexico in a minute."

They were both staring at each other when a shot rang out from the edge of the compound. Ortega jumped up from his heavy chair. He was grabbing for his pistol when the door swung open and a guard burst into the room. "It's Captain Portolá," he said. "They're coming down the hill."

Sergeant Ortega rubbed his face with relief. "Thank God," he said. Both the priest and the sergeant were standing in the open doorway when Captain Portolá rode through the compound gate. They stared at each other in dismay as one by one the ragged expedition members came into the stockade. All of the men were soaked to the skin. Their boots were heavy with mud. It was all too obvious that the men were hungry, exhausted, and cold. The earlier cheering by Ortega's men turned to silence as Portolá's troops passed through the gate and it was seen that the packs on the mules were empty. Some of the animals had two packs on their backs, indicating that some of the pack animals had died. Captain Portolá stopped his horse in front of Ortega's office and tied it to a hitching post. Don Fernando Rivera and Pedro Fages tied up their horses next to the captain's and they all walked into the office.

Sergeant Ortega studied his superior: he looked haggard, much thinner than he had been months before. "Captain, it is good to see you. Come sit by my fire."

Captain Portolá and his officers took off their wet wraps and sat in chairs beside the flames. Father Serra also studied the captain's mood for a moment. "Did you find Monterey?" the padre asked.

"No," Portolá answered, clenching his fists.

"You mean that you would go to Rome and miss seeing the Pope?"

The captain sighed with exasperation. "We have failed to locate Monterey, Padre, but we have found San Francisco to be more than anyone ever dreamed of."

Sergeant Ortega sat down in his chair. "Our situation is desperate here, Captain. We are almost out of supplies and the San Antonio has not been sighted."

Portolá looked up at the sergeant. "We had to eat some of our mules on the journey and you are almost out of supplies? Well, we tried! History will give us credit for that much at least."

Father Serra rose to his feet. "You're not suggesting that we give up, are you, Captain?"

"Do we have any other choice?"

Father Serra reflected for a moment. "I'll stay here by myself if I must."

The captain yawned. "Do as you wish, Padre. I haven't the energy to argue with you."

Lieutenant Pedro Fages sighed and shook his head. "We have searched every inch of ground between here and San Francisco and Monterey does not exist!"

The captain turned to Fages. "Don't argue with the Padre, you'll never win." He groaned and added, "I should know."

Father Serra extended his hands and turned to the captain. "I'm not an unreasonable man. I just know for certain that the San Antonio will be here."

Lieutenant Rivera leaned forward in his chair. "In time to bury us before the vultures pick our bones."

The captain laughed. "Do you see what I mean, Pedro?"

"But, Captain," Father Serra insisted, "the King is depending on us to settle this land. San Diego is desperately needed for refitting the galleons from Manila."

Rivera rose to his feet. "I say that we leave!"

"Me too," Fages said.

"If we try to hold out a little longer," Serra insisted, "I know that a ship will come."

Portolá shook his head. "How much longer, Padre?"

"I will begin a Novena in the morning."

"And after your Masses, we will leave in nine days," the captain stated.

Father Serra smiled. "Do what you must, Captain, but I will remain alone if I have to and eat the grass like a beast of burden."

The captain contemplated what Father Serra had said. "If the San

Antonio isn't sighted by Monday, the 19th of March, we turn back."

Father Serra began the series of Masses the next morning and his voice was just as strong, his faith still untouched when he concluded the last of the services on March 19th. He went alone to the top of the hill as the captain ordered his soldiers to prepare for the trip back to Mexico. While the troops carried out the captain's order, Father Serra knelt in solemn prayer all afternoon. He was still there, praying, as daylight faded. Portolá saw the lonely figure in prayer and waited until it was nearly dark. Only the western sky showed any light as the captain stopped in front of Father Serra. He removed his hat and held it in his hand. "You know what day this is, Padre."

Father Serra released his heavy crucifix. "March 19th, the feast of St. Joseph."

"It's our last day in upper California."

"The day isn't over yet, Captain," he said as he looked at the rapidly narrowing band of light in the west.

"We must leave in the morning, Padre. Do as you will," the captain said as he turned away.

"I shall stay aboard the *San Carlos* and wait, if God wills it. Captain Canizares has given me his permission."

"I will leave you to your prayers," Portolá said. He began descending the hill to the stockade. Once he looked back, troubled, and saw the little, old priest with his arms outstretched in prayer. Against the backlight, he looked like a cross.

Portolá had almost reached the gate when he heard Father Serra calling. Thinking that the priest was in trouble, he started back at a run. The sun had disappeared completely and the captain could barely make out the figure of the padre. Father Serra was pointing out across the water. "There she is, Captain! It's the *San Antonio*!" the little priest yelled at the top of his voice.

A disbelieving Portolá stopped at the padre's side and peered at the darkening waters. Something was there all right. Crosses? No! No! Ship's masts! A smile softened the officer's face and the two men embraced. "Indeed, you are right, Padre!"

The captain drew his pistol from its holster and fired a shot into the air. He waved his arms over his head and some of the soldiers came running toward the vantage point with their muskets in hand. "See for yourself," the captain yelled. "The *San Antonio* has come . . . just as Father Serra said she would."

Every man capable of walking converged on the hill where they, too, sighted the top sails of the small ship on the horizon. The expedition was jubilant and they began to shout and dance in circles around each other.

"We shall now find Monterey with our replenished supplies!" the captain exclaimed, then fell silent and knelt beside his men who, one by one, had fallen to their knees to join the little priest in solemn prayer.

CHAPTER IV

APTAIN Gaspár de Portolá went overland to Monterey in his second attempt to find the bay that Sebastian Vizcaíno had written about in 1603. This time he was successful. Father Junípero Serra arrived a week later, on June 3, 1770, aboard the *San Antonio*, which was captained by Juan Perez. Early in the morning, Father Serra was greeted on the ship by Captain Portolá. They were then transported to the shore in a small boat, along with Captain Perez.

Father Serra was captivated by the beauty of the rugged coastline as the dinghy cut through the small waves. If the oaks had been olive trees, the landscape would have been much the same as his beloved Mallorca. The boat was beached with the help of several soldiers. Father Serra walked directly to a massive oak tree and stopped. Perez and Portolá were close behind. "Here I shall offer Mass, under the same old oak tree where the Carmelites celebrated their safe arrival in 1603 with Sebastian Vizcaíno," he told them.

Two soldiers carried a large, bronze bell they had taken from the small boat. "Where do you want us to put this?" one asked Father Serra.

The priest pointed to a branch of the oak tree. "Hang it on a lower limb where it can be reached," he said, "and construct the altar near the base of the tree."

One soldier climbed up into the tree and the other threw him a rope that was attached to the bell. Several other soldiers helped hold the heavy bronze up in the air while it was secured. Captains Perez and Portolá watched at a distance and they were amazed that Father Serra had so much energy. "The padre nearly died on the road between Velicata and San Diego," Portolá said to Perez.

Juan Perez folded his arms across his chest. "You'd never know it by the look of him now."

Portolá smiled. "The people in Madrid will be dancing in the streets and it's not because of me."

Perez sounded perplexed. "What do you mean, Captain?"

The captain rubbed at his beard. "If it weren't for that stubborn, old man over there . . . and his faith . . . I would have returned to Mexico."

Father Serra walked over to the edge of the water and sat down on a rock. He looked out across the bay and watched the *San Antonio* as it lay at anchor. "So much to do and so little time to do it," he thought sadly.

Sensing some of the padre's emotions, Captain Portolá went over to the priest who looked up at his approach. "Am I interrupting your prayer, Padre?"

Father Serra extended his hand. "No, Captain. Sit down here beside me. We both can admire the beauty."

Captain Portolá complied with the padre's wishes. After a moment, he said, "You know that I am to be replaced now, don't you, Padre?"

"By whom?" the padre asked in disbelief.

"By Lieutenent Pedro Fages."

Father Serra clasped the soldier's hand. "May God grant you as much success in future assignments."

"You know as well as I do, Padre, who's responsible for this magnificent success."

"The Master we both serve," Father Serra said proudly.

Captain Portolá sighed. "The truth of the matter will come out in time but I've learned not to argue with you, my friend."

"I will say nothing but the truth. It was you, Captain, who convinced the others to wait. I had nothing to do with it."

"Your friars are all educated men, Padre. And they write letters after their evening prayers."

Father Serra shook his head. "I have no control over that. Let them write what they will," he said, "but I wish that there be no mention made of me, except in relation to the blunders I may have committed."

Captain Portolá smiled and reached out and placed his hand on Father Serra's shoulder. "I wanted to give you a warning before I leave."

"What is it, Captain?"

Captain Portolá looked very serious. "Watch out for Pedro Fages. You must understand that I wouldn't say this unless I were truly concerned for the mission effort here in upper California."

"Go ahead, my son."

"Fages is a thief and he's stricken with greed. He has been filling his personal chests with the provisions that the doctor set aside for the sick."

"Do you have evidence?"

"I've seen him myself," Portolá insisted. "That's why you should relocate the mission down by the river where I camped while I waited for your arrival."

Father Serra nodded his head as he listened intently.

"The land is fertile and there is a large tribe of Indians there who are very peaceful and generous. They gave us venison for our celebration."

"That is a good sign."

"I think that the farther you are from Fages, the better."

"Thank you, Captain. I shall consider your advice. If things are as you say, I shall write to Viceroy Bucareli and request that the Mission San Carlos be relocated near the mouth of the river."

"I feel better now that I have said this. I can travel in peace when the tide is right."

"I hope you join in the celebration, my son, for it will be a joyous day that will long be remembered."

Father Serra walked to where the altar had been prepared. He put on an alb and a stole and began a Mass. When the service was concluded, he blessed the cross that lay on the ground and the multitude cheered when it was raised into position. Muskets were fired, the bell was rung, and the cannon on the *San Antonio* thundered loudly. A soldier came forward with the colors of Spain and the pole was stuck into the sand near the cross. The large group began to chant over and over again, "Long live the Faith! Long live the King!"

Captain Portolá walked to the flag with a handful of dirt in his raised hand. "I claim this land for Charles III, the King of Spain!"

The muskets were fired, the bell was rung, and the cannon of the *San Antonio* roared out again. The cheering started all over again and continued until Father Serra raised his hands and began to speak. "May God bless all who inhabit this land and all who will ever inhabit it!"

The participants broke ranks and began to feast on the great banquet that had been prepared. Roast beef, venison, and lamb were being turned on spits. Tables were set with many delicacies and a steward began to pour cups of red wine from large skins and casks.

Father Serra walked a short distance away where he sat to watch the people celebrate. Their joy was like music to his ears and he smiled at so many people enjoying themselves after enduring so many hardships in San Diego.

Suddenly he sensed someone near him. "Captain Portolá," he said, "why aren't you celebrating with the others?"

"I came for your blessing, Father. I have been blessed many times but this one, my friend, I shall remember always." He looked down at his soldiers who were now at peace. Their bellies were full and they were safe once more. Then he dropped to his knees as the crucifix was held out to him by the little priest who had the heart of a giant.

San Luis Obispo de Tolosa

CHAPTER V

IEUTENANT Pedro Fages took charge after Captain Portolá had departed aboard the *San Antonio*. As predicted, he cut back on the soldiers' rations and worked them from daylight to dark. When winter came, the working conditions were difficult at best. It was windy and cold and the wet ground was slippery with mud. It wasn't long until the hospital tents were full of sick men who were coughing with pneumonia but that was no escape from the long details. Fages himself made the rounds through the hospital and forced the men back outside into the elements, with threats of further ration cuts and public lashings.

One night, as the rain pounded on the roof, Pedro Fages sat at his desk studying large sheets of building plans. A warm fire was burning in the fireplace, several oil paintings were hanging on the walls, and comfortable chairs lined the inside of the small building that had been erected for use as a temporary office. When a soldier walked into the room, Lieutenant Fages looked up from his work. "Come in, Corporal," he said. "Tell me how things are going."

The man stood at attention. "I think we're ahead of schedule, sir."

"We'd be doing better if some of our soldiers weren't helping the padres. Am I right?"

"Yes, sir!"

Fages smiled. "At ease, Corporal. Warm yourself by my fire. Stay and have supper with me."

The man stood at ease. "If that is your wish, sir."

"Tomorrow you will tell the soldiers that if they are caught helping the padres they will be flogged!"

"Yes, sir!"

Fages leaned back in his chair. "I told Father Serra today that his whole plan is a joke. He doesn't even know how to lay out a cemetery, much less a mission."

The corporal shook his head. "I don't know about that man. I saw him working in the mud like a common laborer today, carrying logs and mixing mortar."

Fages laughed. "He's a fool. A man in his position need not soil his hands."

There was a knock on the door. When the corporal answered it, Father Serra stepped inside out of the driving rain. He removed the hood from his head and shook the water from his garments. Pedro Fages rose to his feet and smiled ingratiatingly at the padre. "We were just discussing how hard you've been working lately, Padre. Please do sit down."

Father Serra declined the offer. "What I have to say is important, Lieutenant."

"Be seated. Tell me what's on your mind."

Father Serra took a seat. "I have noticed that many of your men do not go to church on Sundays."

"Perhaps they have better things to do with their time."

"Is it true that you have been working them, including the sick, six days a week and reserving Sundays to get ready for Monday-morning inspection?"

Some of the humor went out of the lieutenant's voice. "That is not your concern, Padre. It's a military matter."

"The spiritual well-being of everyone in this territory is exactly my concern."

Fage's expression hardened. "I am in charge here, Padre. You would be wise not to forget it."

"I intend to write to the Viceroy if this practice isn't stopped. The men shall work five days, as the law provides, and have Saturday to clean their uniforms for Monday-morning inspection."

"Is that all you have to say, Padre?"

"No, Lieutenant. There's another matter," Father Serra said as he slipped his hood back onto his head and stood. "The sick should be allowed to get their rest or they may never recover."

There was another knock on the door. The corporal opened it and several soldiers brought in platters of hot food. They placed everything on the table while the lieutenant rolled up the plans. The servants uncovered the platters and revealed steaming quantities of vegetables, roast beef, fresh bread, and several desserts. Fages looked over at Father Serra. "Would you care to join us?" he asked. "You look thin, as if you could use a good meal."

Father Serra walked to the door. "No, thank you. My colleagues are waiting for me." He walked out of the small office, returning to the rain and the darkness.

Pedro Fages began to pile the food onto his plate. "Help yourself, Corporal. The warehouse is bulging with food."

The corporal sat down at the table. "I think that the Father Presidente is going to be trouble."

Fages smiled as he raised his glass. "Oh, well, I think he's met his match!"

The corporal touched glasses, then joined in Fages' laughter and the two men began to eat and drink. Neither knew, nor cared, that outside the other soldiers were grumbling. The smell of food, good wholesome food, was tormenting them. They were hungry and trouble was brewing, just as Portolá had warned.

After his confrontation with Lieutenant Fages, Father Serra realized that there was no way he could ever hope to communicate with such a man. Other actions were called for.

He went directly to his quarters and wrote a letter to Viceroy Bucareli. The padre signed the letter in his usual way: "This most unworthy priest, Fr. Junípero Serra."

Compared to Fages' luxurious surroundings, Father Serra's quarters were meager. The room was furnished with a wooden desk, a hardwood chair, and a bed made of two rough-hewn planks covered by a single blanket. A crucifix hung on the wall and a small candle sat on the desk. The padre picked up the candle and dripped some wax on the letter he had just completed and stamped a seal on it. He was blowing on the wax when a knock came at his door and a young friar entered.

Juan Crespí, Serra's former student, asked, "You wanted to see me, Father Presidente?"

Father Serra leaned back in his chair and rubbed at his legs, which had been bothering him again in the damp weather. "While I go to found the Mission San Antonio, you will be in charge here."

"What would you have me do?"

"Take all that you can from this place and prepare to build the Mission San Carlos where Captain Portolá suggested. I have written a letter to the Viceroy. Soon we will have his permission, I am almost certain."

"I will take care of everything."

"All we can do, until we have the authority, is raise the cross and accumulate materials."

"I shall do as you ask, Padre."

"It will give us a chance to make contact with the Indians who live there. I shall bless the cross when I return."

Father Serra and Fathers Pieras and Sitjar set out for a place that was covered with scrub oak trees on the east slopes of the Santa Lucia Mountains. By the time they arrived, Father Serra was limping badly, dragging his leg behind him. He didn't complain, however, and he brushed off questions about his health. The three priests raised the cross in the usual manner and the ringing of the bronze bell could be heard for miles.

The soldiers and the padres worked for a week, constructing a corral for the animals, and erecting the first of the mission buildings. One by one, the timid Indians began to visit and Father Serra gave them gifts of dates, nuts, and bread, along with colored beads. There was joy in his eyes as he blessed each one who came for the presents.

By now his leg had worsened to the point that he was forced to ride a mule from San Antonio Mission to the place he had told Father Crespí to begin work at Carmel. The tall cross could be seen when his party was still a great distance away. A group of Indians were seen at work, limbing some trees. Other Indians were making hand-hewn beams and stacking them into large piles.

The sound of ringing axes was heard everywhere as Serra climbed painfully down from the mule and embraced his friend. "Father Juan Crespí!"

Juan smiled in pride and pointed to the stockpiles. "It is going well, Padre."

"I see that it is. We will be ready to build as soon as we have permission."

"Captain Portolá was correct about the helpfulness of the Indians."

Father Serra's glance fell on a young Indian boy who was working with an older native. They were both clad in breech cloths and wearing bright colored headbands with black crest feathers from California partridges. A stab of memory made the little priest draw his breath sharply and he saw in his mind the rain-slick mound of earth inside the mission walls at San Diego. "Who is the boy?" he asked Father Crespí.

"A local youth. He and his father have been most helpful."

Father Serra wiped away a tear that ran down his cheek. "He looks so much like my José Maria."

"Shall I bring him to you, Padre?"

"No, Juan. I shall go to him myself," he said, turning and limping toward the boy who was busy chopping the limbs from a fallen pine tree. The youth looked up and smiled shyly. Father Serra touched the boy on the forehead and blessed him as the boy's father watched. Tears were streaming down the little priest's face when he returned to Father Crespí. Behind him, just as José Maria had done two years before, the boy followed like a small shadow.

Father Serra took a cup from the saddlebag that hung across the mule's back. He filled it with the water from a skin, blessed it, and sprinkled it on the cross and said a prayer in Latin. The boy watched the proceedings, then tried to imitate the way the priest made the sign of the cross.

"Well, it's a start anyway," Father Serra said.

Over the next year Father Serra and the young boy became very close. They worked and studied together while the padre waited for the Viceroy's letter to arrive by ship. Serra taught the young boy how to make beams from the trees they cut and later taught him how to speak Spanish. Soon

26

the lad wanted to know how to read and write and the priest became his tutor. The boy was baptized after he had received all of his religious instruction and he was named Juan Evangelista.

At the Presidio, soldiers were still working under very harsh conditions. Their rations continued to be withheld on the slightest whim of Fages and they were living on whatever they could catch: rats, snakes, and coyotes. Some of them, near desperation, deserted their posts. Others joined them, especially after Pedro Fages and his corporal rode out accompanying Father Serra to found Mission San Luis Obispo.

After San Luis Obispo was established, they continued southward toward San Diego with Pedro Fages and his troops leading the way. Father Serra and Juan rode close behind on mules. Near the end of the third week, the little priest pulled up on the reins of his mule. "Listen," he said. The sound of ringing hammers and axes could be heard in the distance. Curious, he rode up beside Fages and asked, "What is that noise? We are still quite far from San Diego."

Fages merely stared at him while continuing to ride. "Didn't I tell you, Padre? No ... I guess I didn't. The Mission San Gabriel has been founded."

"Why wasn't I told of this?

"Surely the Father Presidente doesn't need to know everything."

"We were to found Mission San Buenaventura next. That is what the Viceroy ordered."

Fages laughed. "You worry too much, Padre."

When the party entered the compound they saw many Indians working alongside the soldiers. Father Cambon, who was instructing some of the Indian children, looked up to greet the lieutenant and Father Serra.

Pedro Fages dismounted and his corporal led both of their horses to a small corral.

"Our work goes well," Father Cambon told the lieutenant.

The smile was not returned. Fages looked around the compound. "Why are so many Indians inside these walls?"

"But ... you don't understand!" Cambon said. "They have helped so much. And they have brought their children ... to be instructed in the Faith."

"There should be no more than five adults inside of these walls at any time!" the officer snapped.

"But these are the most peaceful Indians in all of California!"

The corporal came back to stand beside Pedro Fages.

"Five can stay," Fages said, "but the rest must leave. See to it, Corporal."

"Yes, sir!" the corporal answered. He pointed to several soldiers to form a detail.

The troops grabbed the unarmed Indians, pushing and shoving them out of the stockade, while the frightened children gathered around Father Serra and Juan Evangelista. Angry, Fages went into a small building and slammed the door.

Father Cambon was shocked. He was shaking his head mournfully as he walked over to Father Serra. "All of our work has just been undone," he said.

Father Serra watched as the last of the adults were expelled from the stockade. Suddently, as if realizing they were being left alone, the children screamed and ran after their parents. Young Juan Evangelista watched in obvious distress.

The corporal looked grim as he walked past the padres and entered the office where Pedro Fages was sitting. The soldier paused a moment, cleared his throat, and said, "Sir, I know that you long to be Governor of California someday but I fear when the Viceroy hears of this . . ."

Fages interrupted. "I shall write the Viceroy and blame any setbacks on the twelve Franciscans and the Father Presidente, who has urged so many of my men to desert!"

"I am only thinking of you, Lieutenant."

Fages scratched at the side of his chin as he paused, deep in thought. "Things are running so smoothly in these missions that the Viceroy might decide not to appoint a governor."

"What do you have in mind?"

"I will leave you here with a lot of wine and brandy." He smiled but there was no humor in his eyes. "The rest is up to you."

"I know exactly what to do, sir."

"Yes, I thought you might," he laughed.

Father Serra appeared at the open door and Fages looked up. "You are just the man I wanted to see, Padre."

"Did you want to discuss the founding of Mission San Buenaventura?"

"No, Padre." he shrugged. "I wanted to tell you that the soldiers here are going to be replaced."

Father Serra was surprised. "But they are doing a splendid job. Haven't you seen the progress?"

"My men will do even better," Fages said as he pointed to his corporal.

The soldier was grinning as Father Serra walked out of the office.

Fages spoke softly. "I shall check on your progress when I return from San Diego. I must be there when the supplies are unloaded from the *San Antonio*. We don't want the Father Presidente to get more than his share."

The two men stared at each other knowingly, then began to laugh.

As Pedro Fages led the expedition south, Father Serra sent a message to Juan Crespí, by courier, asking him to come to San Diego and take the supplies back to Monterey as quickly as he could. While Serra waited for the arrival of the *San Antonio*, he met and talked with his many colleagues who were stationed at Mission San Diego. Crespí arrived and joined the other Franciscans. For Father Serra it was a time to reflect on what they had accomplished. A lesser man would have been satisfied, even proud! And yet the little priest realized that their work had only just begun. He was standing at a window listening to the children singing when Father Juan Crespí walked into the room at Mission San Diego.

"I am ready to take the supplies back to Mission San Carlos," Father Juan said. "I would have left yesterday but the Lieutenant . . ."

Father Serra leaned on the edge of his desk. "I know, Juan. But the supplies are needed at the missions right away and I must go to Mexico City and meet with the Viceroy."

"But, my friend, that is a journey of over fifteen-hundred miles. And you haven't been well lately."

"I shall take young Juan with me. Please inform his parents that our journey will take us farther than we had planned."

Crespí moved closer to Father Serra. "I beg you to reconsider this journey, for I fear that I will never see you again."

The little priest picked up a stack of letters from his desk. "You will be too busy to be concerned about me, my dear friend. The Viceroy has given his permission to build the Mission San Carlos near the river."

Father Juan reflected for a moment. "He seems to be a reasonable man."

"I shall pray that he is."

Father Crespí looked at the large stack of letters. "And the other news, Padre?"

Father Serra picked up his glasses and put them on. "Father Palóu has written and told me of a rumor concerning a possible Dominican takeover of the upper California missions."

"That's preposterous!"

Father Serra shuffled through the letters and extracted a short note.

"What most concerns me is this message from Father Cambon."

"What has happened at Mission San Gabriel?"

"It was attacked by Indians and it has been abandoned."

"What was the reason?"

Father Serra removed his glasses. "The corporal who was left in charge by Lieutenant Fages has been encouraging indecent acts upon the Indian women ever since I left."

Crespí buried his face in his hands and sighed in obvious frustration. "Holy Mother of God!"

Serra's eyes began to glisten with tears. "The soldiers there raped and killed the wife of the chief," he said. "When he went to confront the corporal, he was killed. His head was put on a pole outside the stockade so all could see."

"That's horrible!"

"And even worse is the fact that the chief had left his son with Father

Cambon that very morning. The boy witnessed the entire proceedings."

"My God!"

"So you see why I must make this journey, Juan. Pedro Fages is coming between God and his children. And I, as the Father Presidente, have the responsibility to correct this abomination, even if I should die on the way."

"The Lieutenant has ordered you not to leave the country."

Serra reached out and placed his hand gently on Father Crespí's shoulder. "So I have heard. But I have made arrangements with the captain of the *San Carlos* to sail for San Blas on the morning tide. I shall go to the ship soon and begin a letter that young Juan can deliver to the Viceroy . . . ," he paused for a moment, then completed the sentence, "in case God wills that I do not complete my journey."

"All of us are in complete agreement that something must be done. We shall pray for the success of your mission," Father Juan said calmly. "And I shall work hard to get Mission San Carlos ready for your return."

There was a light knock on the door. When Crespí opened it, young Juan entered the room with a bouquet of pink roses in his hand. He handed them to Father Serra and smiled. "Look what I found growing on the hillside today. I know they're your favorite, Padre."

Father Serra smiled as he received the gift. "It is just what I needed, Juan, to lift my spirit before our long journey."

The next morning, the *San Carlos* set sail. It was still visible in the distance when an angry Lieutenant Fages rode up to the dock and saw the ship heading for open water. He climbed down from his horse and yelled at the men who were working there. "Has anyone here seen the Father Presidente?"

Some of the men shook their heads, others continued stacking boxes and ignored Fages.

"Was he on board the *San Carlos*?"

The men working on the dock remained silent. Fages paced back and forth in frustration. "Look at this, sir," a soldier exclaimed, coming out from behind a stack of crates.

"What is it?" Fages asked, turning.

The soldier handed the lieutenant a single rose. "I found this lying on the dock," he said, "and everyone knows that Father Serra loves flowers, especially the Rose of Castile."

Lieutenant Fages looked out at the ship again. "Get out of my sight!" he screamed. "All of you."

The soldiers climbed on their horses and rode away quickly. Pedro Fages walked to the edge of the dock with the rose in his gloved hand. He closed his fist, squeezing tightly, and threw the flower into the water. "Damn you, Junípero! I have the authority in California, not you!"

Lieutenant Fages straightened up and wiped his brow with his sleeve. "To think that a lover of children and a lover of flowers would try to bring me down." He paused. "The fool! It's insane!"

Pedro Fages looked down at the flower. It fell apart in the rough water; the petals separated from the bud and little bits of pink drifted away in different directions.

Fages shuddered. Father Serra was like the wild flower. Small, needing no nourishment except for what God gave, rugged and enduring. Oh yes, he could crush the little priest just as he had the rose but, like the flower in the water, somehow the color, the seeds — Serra's love, Serra's belief, Serra's devotion — would drift away only to be redeposited on the shore where they would take root again.

Fages' stare went back to the ship under sail. He knew then that, in addition to this anger and frustration with the padre, there was some other emotion growing in his chest. He recognized it for what it was and suppressed it: a grudging admiration . . .

❧

San Antonio de Padua

CHAPTER VI

ATHER SERRA and Juan Evangelista arrived in San Blas on a bright, sunny day. They walked across the dock and down a flower-lined path. A ship was on a set of blocks, under construction and nearly completed, but no one worked on her.

A man was sitting near the base of a tree. He held the reins of a small donkey in his massive hands. A pack on the animal's back contained carpenter's tools. When Father Serra saw that the man seemed to be in distress, he limped over to his side and asked, "Is something troubling you, my son?"

The man looked up and saw the little priest and the boy. He jumped to his feet immediately. "Excuse me, Padre. I didn't see you coming or I would have greeted you."

Father Serra placed his hand on the tall man's shoulder. "You seem to be very upset. Can I help?"

"I am Hernando Garcia. You must be the famous Father Presidente from the new colony!"

"How did you know, my son?"

"Your fame precedes you, Padre. Everyone in Mexico has heard of your work."

Father Serra tried to ignore the praise. "You seem to have a burden. What can I do to help?"

"I build ships, Padre. And I have heard that the port here in San Blas is to be closed down. I am worried about how I will feed my children."

"How many children do you have?"

"Ten, Padre. And they're all fine children of God, I might add."

"Are you working on that large ship, the *Santiago*?"

"Yes, but I hear it is to be burned before it is completed."

"There is nothing to worry about," Father Serra said. "That is part of

33

the reason my young friend and I are on our way to Mexico City, to prevent such an atrocity."

"You don't intend to walk all the way to Mexico City, do you Padre? You are already limping."

"I know of no other way to get there, my son."

Garcia smiled and handed the reins to young Juan. "I will give you the loan of my donkey. She is as gentle as a kitten."

"But I may not come back this way for a long time, my friend."

Garcia removed the pack from the small animal's back. "It's the least I can do for a man who serves the Lord," he said with a broad smile. "Especially since he's also the man who might save my job!"

Garcia helped the priest climb onto the donkey. Father Serra looked over at him. "I shall pray for you and your family for the rest of my life."

"Your blessings are most welcome, Padre."

"You must work faster, Hernando, so this vessel is completed. I am in no mind to be defeated." He paused and thought. "I shall return to San Diego on the *Santiago* when it leaves with its first cargo."

Garcia waved as Juan led the donkey down the path. "May God go with you, Padre Serra."

The journey had not promised to be an easy one, nor was it. By the end of the first day, Father Serra was grimacing in pain each time the donkey stumbled or attempted to trot. The padre's leg was infected again but he kept silence as Juan led the small animal up the steep mountain path. Here the vegetation was lush and green and it glistened with light reflected in the raindrops left by a recent shower. Juan stumbled once and fell. Although he denied being ill, it became obvious that the boy was tired, weak and feverish. Soon he was wiping the perspiration from his face and he shivered uncontrollably.

When Father Serra realized that young Juan had fallen ill, he dismounted from the donkey and insisted that the protesting youth ride. Father Serra urged the animal along, pulling hard on the rope. He paid no heed to his own leg, which throbbed with each agonizing step. Finally reaching the mountain pass, Father Serra could see a mission church in the distance below. Some of the friars working in the fields saw the pair approaching and dropped their tools and ran to meet them. They half-carried the old man along and led the donkey with the now unconscious boy to their quarters, were both Serra and Juan were placed in beds.

When Father Serra regained consciousness, he found himself in a room made of adobe. A small desk, a chair, and two beds were the only furniture. A crucifix hung on the bare wall; a dim light was supplied by an oil lamp. Juan was covered with many blankets in an effort to break his fever. A Franciscan priest, one of many who had been in attendance day and night, wiped the boy's face with a cool, damp cloth. Father Serra, also covered with blankets, was lying on a bed across the room. The little priest held his crucifix firmly as he prayed. There was just enough light to see his torment, the sadness in his eyes, and the movement of his lips.

"I am content to die, oh Lord," he prayed, "feeling that I have already accomplished what you want of me, but spare the boy, I beseech you. If he dies in this land, his parents will think that their son was killed by Spaniards and our trust will be broken again." Father Serra paused as his body shuddered with the alternating chills and fever. A friar came to his side and cooled his face with a damp cloth. "Please rest, Padre. You are very ill."

Father Serra held tightly to his crucifix. "Please spare my friend, who has helped me to do your work with so much love and devotion."

"I beg you to save your energy, Padre," the priest whispered. "Do you realize that you have been unconscious for three days and have been given the last rites?"

Father Serra didn't answer. He threw the blankets aside, staggered from the bed, and settled down on his knees before the crucifix on the wall. He still burned with fever as he made the sign of the cross and continued to pray. It was almost midnight when the attendant left the room, closing the door softly so the padre's devotions would not be disturbed.

The little priest prayed until the morning light shone brightly through the small window. The padre's concentration was so deep that he didn't notice Juan stirring from his sleep. The boy climbed out of bed, his clothing soaked with heavy perspiration, and stared at the kneeling priest. "Good morning, Padre," he said softly.

Startled, Father Serra turned his head and faced the Indian youth. "Praise the Lord, my son. You have been so ill that I feared for your life!" he said, making the sign of the cross and rising painfully to his feet.

Juan went to the padre's side and the old man hugged him. The boy helped his friend back into bed and covered him with several blankets. "I feel wonderful, Padre. You get well and we will continue our journey."

Father Serra nodded his head as Juan left the room. The priest who attended them was asleep on a small cot in the hallway. He awakened and shook his head in disbelief when he saw the boy.

"Father Serra will be resting for a couple of days," the youth said, "then we will be off to see the Viceroy!"

The priest was speechless as he blessed himself with the sign of the cross.

Father Serra was still showing signs of his illness three months later when Juan led the padre to San Fernando College, where many of Father Serra's colleagues lived and worked.

Father Verger, the Guardian, embraced the little priest as he climbed down from the donkey.

"The business I have come to attend is most urgent," Father Serra said. "Therefore, I request that my young friend, Juan, be allowed to wait here in your care until I return."

Father Verger smiled. "By all means, Padre. But don't you think that you should rest before you see the Viceroy?"

"His Excellency is expecting me," Father Serra said, "and many of his subjects wait for his decisions."

"When you get back I insist that you rest."

"I have already rested too long, Father Guardian."

Father Serra went directly to the Viceroy's office and was taken to see Bucareli immediately. Entering the large room through a massive doorway, the padre saw a man seated at a desk beside a long row of windows. The Spanish flag was displayed on the wall behind him along with a map of Mexico, Baja California, and the new colony in upper California. Ribbons showed the five missions already established and the Mission San Buenaventura, which had not yet been founded.

The servant announced, "Padre Junípero Serra, the Father Presidente of the upper California missions to see you, your Excellency."

Father Serra limped slowly into the large office. The walls were covered with rows of books and the fireplace was large enough to stand in. The Viceroy rose to his feet. "Come in and be seated, Padre Serra."

Father Serra moved painfully across the tiled floor. With a sigh, he sat down in a chair and pulled a letter from the sleeve of his habit. He held it firmly in his hand. "What I have to say to you, your Excellency, needs your immediate consideration."

"Please proceed."

"The conditions in the missions of upper California could indeed be much better than they are. If you could remove the obstacles that I will endeavor to explain to you, and grant what I ask, there may yet be a chance to convert these people and obtain a beautiful colony for the King."

"Your Guardian at San Fernando had kept me well informed."

"The first two matters are of extreme importance," he said. "The port of San Blas should be retained because bringing supplies overland would be more costly and much more hazardous than sending them in ships."

"I see," the Viceroy said, noncommittally. "Continue."

"It troubles me to tell you that theft, the violation of women, and murder are commonplace occurences in this land without civil law."

"I have studied all of the reports carefully."

Father Serra put the letter he had in his hand on the Viceroy's desk. "Famine is an everyday problem in the colony. That is why the *Santiago* should be completed," he said. "It will be a large ship and will be able to carry the cargo of the *San Antonio* and the *San Carlos* combined. I have written this memorandum to explain this matter in detail."

"I will study your report carefully and will let you know of my decision as soon as possible."

Father Serra paused, studying the man before him. He was sure he knew the Viceroy but, if he had misjudged the official's reaction, a great deal would be lost with this next request. Nonetheless, it needed to be said. "I have done a considerable amount of thinking on other points, such as the replacement of Pedro Fages as the Commandant of Monterey."

Bucareli sat back in his chair. "Who would you suggest as a replacement?"

"The best man in California is Sergeant José Francisco Ortega."

The Viceroy smiled. "If I appointed a sergeant as Commandant, the officers would rebel."

"I understand politics, your Excellency. They can be very inhibiting."

"But I'm inclined to agree with you, Padre Serra. Something must be done."

"Furthermore, your Excellency, I believe that the colonization of this fertile land should be encouraged. The soldiers should be given a payment of land, livestock, and money if they marry Christian Indian women," he said. "Tradesmen should be brought to teach the young Indian boys the necessary skills that keep a colony alive and productive. The Indian people are highly skilled. Their pottery and basket-work is extraordinary."

"You mentioned civil protection for the Indians?"

"Yes, your Excellency, this is most important. Since they are loyal subjects of the King, they should have the protection of his laws. As it is now, if we do not lock the women up at night, they are not safe even in the missions."

Viceroy Bucareli leaned forward in his chair. "Your points are well taken, Padre Serra. It only remains for us to convince the Junta," he said. "Draw up a memorandum, which you and I will submit. We will stand up for it together."

"You are most kind, your Excellency."

"If it were up to me alone, I'd adopt your proposals before you left my office."

"I am very concerned about the *Santiago*," the Padre said. "I have heard that it is in jeopardy of the torch."

"The final decision must come through this office, Padre, so sleep well while I fight for what is right."

"May God bless you, your Excellency."

"I will see you again when you have drawn up your memorandum."

"Then you will see me very soon," the little priest said with a smile.

"May God continue to give you inspiration and boundless energy."

Viceroy Bucareli rose from his chair and escorted Father Serra to the door. The Viceroy then went back to his desk and studied the letter that Father Serra had left on his desk.

CHAPTER VII

OSING no time, Father Serra went to his room in San Fernando College and began to work on the memorandum that Bucareli had requested. The padre sat at his simple desk, quill in hand, and small spectacles in place. He dipped the pen into an inkwell and titled the first page, "Representación."

Father Serra worked for almost two days writing the thirty-two concise articles that he hoped would become law in upper California. He finished his work at dawn on the second day, blew out the lamp, and hurried down a long hallway and out a side door with the memorandum clutched tightly in his hand. Arriving at Viceroy Bucareli's office, he took a seat near the large desk and waited for the man to awaken.

Bucareli arrived, buttoning his jacket as he walked. "You must have worked day and night, Padre," he said, going to his desk.

The padre smiled. "I am sorry to disturb you so early in the morning, your Excellency, but while I sit here and talk, the needs of the missions go unattended. And the situation only gets worse."

"Will you wait for the Junta to meet or will you go back to Monterey?"

"I will take their decision back with me," he said, "even if it takes months. Some of my letters have been withheld in the past."

"Lieutenant Fages?"

"What I say of this man is for the good of the King's colony. If he is replaced, I pray that he will have an assignment that is worthy of his station and I pray that God goes with him."

Bucareli smiled at the little priest and shook his head in amazement. "How can you feel this way, Padre, after all of the problems that this man has caused?"

"I will always pray for him to amend his ways, your Excellency."

Bucareli nodded. "I have arranged a reception for you and your young traveling companion. It will be held after the Junta has delivered its decision."

"I know that young Juan will represent his people well."

"That's exactly what I had in mind, Padre."

"I'm afraid that most people have the wrong impression of the Indian people. They are intelligent and have a goodness of heart that is rare," Serra said. "Their thievery is only an uncontrollable curiosity about all the strange, new things around them."

"I will inform you of the Junta's decision, just as soon as I have heard from them."

Father Serra rose from his chair. "The people in California will be indebted to you forever, your Excellency."

The Viceroy led the little priest to the door. "Oh, Padre, I almost forgot," Bucareli said, reaching into his jacket pocket and extracting an envelope.

Father Serra was surprised when the Viceroy pressed the package into his hand. "What is this?" he asked.

"Your children have many friends," Bucareli said smiling, "myself included."

"May God bless you, your Excellency. I will purchase books and cloth for the children of Carmel and I will tell them who they can thank for this generosity."

"May the Master we both serve go with you, Father Serra."

Viceroy Bucareli watched the padre limp down the hallway, turn left toward the stairs, and disappear. Then he crossed his office to the window and stood watching, as the limping priest came out of the shadows and, with difficulty, mounted the small donkey. It was obvious that Father Serra was ill and exhausted and yet there was a fire in the man, a very special warmth. "I shall pray for you, Father Serra," the Viceroy said softly as he watched the old man melt into the crowd.

Father Serra rode down the busy streets of Mexico City but he found it difficult to rejoice. He felt that his meeting with Viceroy Bucareli had gone very well but he prayed for God to forgive him whatever he might have overlooked during this crucial encounter.

On his return to San Fernando College, he rode through the gate and found the faithful Juan Evangelista waiting for him. "You look tired, Padre," the lad said with concern. "You must go to your bed."

Father Serra climbed down from the animal's back and smiled. The warm morning sun reflected its light in his bright, clear eyes. "This trip has been worth all the effort, my young friend. The Viceroy is a friend of your people. I believe he will see to it that things get better soon."

"I would like to meet him before we leave."

"You will. He has prepared a reception in your honor."

Juan was surprised. "My honor? Me?"

The padre reached into the sleeve of his garment and extracted an envelope. "Yes, Juan, and he has given us a gift to be used to benefit all of the children in Carmel." Father Serra opened the envelope and counted the money. "Glory to God!" he exclaimed when he realized the amount.

"Is it a lot, Padre?"

"There are twelve-thousand pesos here!" he said. "We can buy music books, cloths, blankets, tools, and seeds." He paused and looked at the boy. "And I hope that you pick out something special for your parents and yourself," he added. "You have earned it with your love and devotion to God."

"How will we carry it all, Padre?"

"When you buy in quantity, the merchants will deliver your goods to any destination," he said, "at least that's what I've been told."

"All the way to San Blas?" the Indian boy was awe-struck.

"All the way to San Blas," Serra repeated laughing. "Let's get started right away. Come!"

Juan followed the padre through the gate and down the street leading to the town market area. The cobblestone streets were crowded with busy shoppers. There was a multitude of goods displayed on both sides of the street. Father Serra stopped and bought a whole tableful of blankets for the new converts he expected to make in California. They looked at more bolts of cloth than young Juan thought existed and Father Serra picked out three large ones, paid for them, and told the man where they were to be delivered. The shopping spree continued past lunch time, until Father Serra realized that the youth was no longer with him.

Juan was in front of a dress shop, staring at a beautiful, white wedding gown made of silk. Small pink roses had been embroidered on the front, above the breast, and a long lace veil was displayed beside it. Father Serra watched the boy from a distance; he could see that Juan was mesmerized by the dress. Several minutes passed before the Indian youth rejoined the priest.

Father Serra stopped a passing donkey cart that had oranges for sale, a fruit Juan had never seen before. The merchant gave two oranges to the padre and refused payment. Curious, Juan watched as Father Serra peeled the fruit, then he tried to peel his own. The juice ran down the boy's face and his eyes lit up with pleasure as he tasted the sweetness.

In spite of the urgency of the matter, it took a long time for the Junta to deliberate the Viceroy's message. Father Serra spent his time at study and Juan helped the friars work in their gardens.

It was late one night, almost a year after their arrival, when Father Serra was informed of the Junta's decision. He was reading a book when he heard a light knock on his door and was startled from his deep concentration. Father Verger opened the door slowly and peeked into the room. He had a letter in his hand. "I saw the light from your window," he said softly. "This note from the Viceroy just arrived by special courier."

Father Serra took the letter from the hand of his Guardian. "I've been waiting for this news for a long time."

"Go ahead and read it, Padre. You will not rest until you do."

Serra broke the seal on the letter, adjusted his glasss and studied the note. The expression on his face changed from weariness to sheer joy.

"What does it say, Padre?"

"The people in California will rejoice! The Junta has approved the

'Representación' with only two minor changes!"

Father Verger sighed in relief. "All of us have prayed for this, both day and night. Congratulations, Father Serra."

"I know you all have prayed," he answered with a smile, "and I have done nothing for you. Therefore this most unworthy priest begs your forgiveness and requests to kiss the sandaled feet of every friar, as a token of my loyalty and affection to the Order of St. Francis."

"All we want from you, my friend, is a complete recovery of your health."

"There's no time for that, Father Guardian. I will remain for the Viceroy's reception tomorrow night and will leave the next morning to take this news back to California."

"I know you well, Junípero. Therefore, I will have a coach ready to take you all the way to San Blas." He paused with a warm smile. "You are in no condition to walk or even ride a donkey."

"I can't do that, Father Guardian. I only borrowed the beast that carried me here. I must return it to a gentleman, a shipbuilder in San Blas."

"I will instruct the driver to take his time to make the journey easier for you. The donkey can be tied to the back."

Father Serra paused in thought. "I will consent to this only because you request it." His face lit up. "And I will be able to reach California with this news a lot faster."

Father Verger's expression changed. "By the way, the Dominicans have taken over in lower California. I pray that they don't get their way and move our Order out of upper California as well."

"They are angels but I wish they would find another place to work."

"Father Crespí has written that all is going well at Mission San Carlos," Verger said, "and Father Francisco Palóu has asked to be transferred to upper California. He is waiting for your return and a permanent assignment."

Father Serra's face softened in memory. "It's been nearly twenty-five years since we were all together. What a joyful reunion it will be!"

Verger smiled. "Another good reason to take the coach."

"All right, but only if the donkey comes with us."

"I am sending Father Mugartequi along, in case you fall too ill to get the boy safely back to his parents, heaven forbid!"

"I welcome Father Mugartequi but I am well. I will remain well, although I may not dance all of the dances tomorrow evening," he added with a mischievous grin.

The Viceroy's party was a great success. Everyone in attendance was impressed with the Indian boy's manners and intelligence. Juan had never before seen such wealth and elegance. He stared in amazement at the large crystal chandeliers, the long tables covered with food, and the well-dressed people dancing to music played by an orchestra.

It never occurred to him that he was being evaluated, as a human being, as a citizen of Spain, as a child of God, and as a representative of his people.

Father Serra knew, however, and his smile widened as it became apparent that the evaluations, for the most part, were favorable.

It was clear to him that he and no one else was if it was that
everything there, with those in that room, were connected in one one
in it. It was plain that if it were a made and no one else would, and
it seemed that it for the eyes were found in

San Gabriel Arcángel

CHAPTER VIII

ATHER Serra emerged from a doorway at San Fernando College with Father Verger at his side. The friars who lived at the college were seated in a row, on top of the retaining wall. Father Serra humbly knelt on the ground to kiss the sandaled feet of each friar, saying a short prayer between each stop. When he finally rose to his feet, he was surrounded by two dozen men clad in the garments of the Franciscan Order. Each of them embraced Father Serra and they helped him into the waiting coach in which Father Mugartequi was already seated. Juan Evangelista, carrying a mysterious white box, climbed in after the little priest. The driver cracked his whip and they were off to San Blas. The black carriage crossed a small bridge and started up a steep hill, with the borrowed donkey trotting behind. Father Mugartequi fell asleep soon after they were on their way.

Juan, holding the white box, sat beside Serra. He stared out of the coach window, pensively watching the tree-studded hillsides and the farm animals grazing in the fields.

"You are so quiet, my son," Father Serra said to the youth. "Is there something on your mind?"

Juan turned his head and smiled. "I think you wore me out, Padre."

Father Serra laughed. "That's impossible, my young friend. I sometimes think of all the things I could do if I had but half your energy."

Juan turned his head and stared out of the window again, this time at the few small houses the coach passed as it made its way down the dirt road. A group of happy, brown-skinned children shouted and chased the carriage.

"Sitting here and looking at you, I realize how much you have grown up since the time we met. You are nearly sixteen now."

The boy remained silent but turned to look at Father Serra again.

The padre smiled as he put his arm around the youth. "You are nearly a grown man and you are having trouble with the things a man feels," he said. "Am I correct?"

Juan was surprised. "Yes, Padre."

"You long to see Terese, your childhood friend?"

"She's my fiancée and she's a Christian girl."

Father Serra laughed. "I have no objections, Juan."

Juan was astonished. "I thought that you always wanted me to be a missionary, like yourself."

Serra held Juan's hand and reassured him. "No, my son. I want only what God wants. Some of us are called to leave our families, others are called to raise strong children to carry out his work."

Tears filled Juan's eyes. "All this time I have been worried that I would disappoint you, Padre."

Father Serra tightened his grip on Juan's hand. "If you had only told me earlier, you would not have had to carry this burden."

"I was hoping that you would preside over the ceremony, Padre. We want to marry next year."

"I am counting on it," Father Serra said with smile. "Now open the box."

"What is it, Padre?"

"You will not find out unless you open it, my son."

Mystified, Juan tore the paper from the box. The sound of rattling paper awakened Father Mugartequi, who sat opposite them rubbing at his eyes and yawning, swaying from side to side with the movements of the coach. He watched as Juan eagerly opened the flaps of the container. Both priests exchanged glances as Juan unfolded the soft wrapping inside. Suddenly, seeing the contents, the boy burst into tears. It was the wedding dress! The same one, with pink embroidered roses, that had hung in the shop window in Mexico City. Father Serra pulled the weeping boy close to him and stroked his jet-black hair. "It's all right, my son."

Father Mugartequi was speechless and confused until the priest explained the situation. "There will be a sacred union soon. My family in California will continue to grow and carry out our work."

The coach continued its journey, passing through small towns, most of them new, finally arriving on the dock at San Blas, where it stopped beside a large, handsome, new ship. The *Santiago* was being loaded with tons of supplies. Father Serra gazed at the newly launched vessel and said a prayer of thanksgiving.

Hernando Garcia was standing near the ship with ten children around him. His wife was at his side, holding a new-born infant. Father Serra saw the carpenter and hurried to greet him. "You are a fine craftsman, Hernando. This is the most splendid vessel in the whole Spanish fleet!"

The man embraced Father Serra. "My dear Father Presidente, you are indeed a prophet."

Father Serra was embarrassed. "Give thanks to God, my son."

"When you asked us to finish this vessel quickly, because you meant to sail back on her, I thought that it would be impossible."

"Sometimes we are allowed to work out our prophecies. The ship, her cargo, and her passengers go where they are needed for God's work."

Juan handed the donkey's reins to the carpenter: the man took them in his massive hands and said, "I pray that she has served you well."

Father Serra smiled. "All men should have the same devotion as this creature."

Hernando Garcia's wife came forward with the infant in her arms. Father Serra lifted the blanket that covered the baby's face.

"We have named him Junípero," the carpenter said with pride.

Father Serra took the child from his mother's arms. He sat down on a small crate and immediately the rest of the children gathered around him. The priest exclaimed at the strength of the baby as the infant grabbed his finger tightly.

"Come away from the padre, children," Mrs. Garcia said. "He is tired from his long journey."

Father Serra looked up at the woman. "Please, let them come to me. I haven't had a chance to sing since I left Monterey."

The mother watched as the little priest began to sing a hymn in perfect key. The children joined in as he directed them, followed by Mr. and Mrs. Garcia. Juan and Father Mugartequi cleared their throats and joined the group and soon the entire San Blas dock was filled with the harmony of their music.

⤳✦⤳

San Juan Capistrano

CHAPTER IX

N the early morning, Father Serra and Juan set sail aboard the *Santiago*. The new vessel was under the command of Captain Juan Perez. Due to unfavorable winds, they were forced to anchor in San Diego Bay on March 13th, 1774. The people of San Diego welcomed the ship because their supplies were very low.

José Ortega had been promoted to the rank of lieutenant. He went to meet Father Serra just as soon as the ship had been tied to the dock. With Juan Evangelista at his side, the padre walked down the gang plank. The two men embraced. "It looks like you did well in Mexico City!"

Father Serra smiled. "You're not doing so badly yourself, my friend."

"I have heard that you had something to do with my promotion, Padre."

"It is your deeds that have earned you new responsibilites, my son."

"It gladdens me to think of how much I can help you now, Padre!"

"You have already done more than I have a right to expect."

"You won't believe the change that has come over Pedro Fages. The Viceroy sent him a message to cooperate with the mission effort and now he has become your collaborator," he said. "The padres here, with his help, are achieving great things."

"Can this be so?" Father Serra questioned aloud. "Fages is to be replaced by Don Fernando Rivera."

"Captain Rivera's men are just idling around the missions and causing trouble."

"The attacks on the Indian people continue?"

"I'm afraid so, Padre. But if any of my men participate, I will lock them up for six months in the guardhouse."

"It gives me peace of mind to know that you are here, for I must get back to Mission San Carlos and see how my old friends are doing."

Lieutenant Ortega looked back at the ship. "The *Santiago* is a splendid vessel. There should never be famine in California again."

"I will pray for that. And I will tell everyone that I meet on my journey that there are supplies waiting in San Diego."

"Why do you rush off? Don't you ever sleep?"

"My traveling companion hasn't seen his fiancée in nearly two years."

*　　*　　*

It was Father Serra who rode at the front of the expedition going overland to Monterey and he was the first to sight the cross at Carmel. He pointed to it and said, "It's a joy to be home," urging the small donkey along as fast as it could trot.

The bell at the mission began to peal. Father Serra rode quickly across the open field which was dotted with a few scrub oak trees. He stopped at the open gate and gazed at the spectacular changes that had taken place in his absence. A group of Indians were tilling the fields and Father Juan Crespí was among them. The padre saw rows of young corn plants six inches tall and a large corral filled with animals.

Most of the buildings had been completed. There were classrooms, a chapel, shops, storage buildings, and living quarters, all finished with a coat of white stucco that had taken on a light brown tint. The entire compound was surrounded by high adobe walls.

The rest of the expedition, consisting of six soldiers, mules, beef and milk cattle, goats, and a few squealing pigs, finally caught up with Father Serra and they followed him through the gate. The people in the mission dropped their work and ran to greet the little priest as word spread of his arrival. Many reached up for his hand and laughing children ran beside him as he blessed them all with the sign of the cross. Juan Evangelista jumped from his donkey to hug both his parents. A beautiful young Indian girl, who was about fifteen years old, also received his embrace.

As Father Serra dismounted, he was received by his two friends, Fathers Crespí and Palóu. It was a poignant reunion. Father Serra held out his hands to them and said, "This progress is amazing, Juan. Praise God!"

"Praise God you have come back to us, my friend!" they replied in unison.

Father Serra turned and faced Palóu. "My prayers have truly been answered," he said with a smile. "My Indian children will benefit tremendously from your zeal, Francisco."

"If you only knew how much I have prayed to be here, all of us working together in this new land!" Father Palóu replied. He stepped aside for Father Crespí, who said, "Come, Padre Serra. I have arranged a surprise for you near your new quarters."

The three priests walked across the compound together as the multitudes began to assemble in church. Father Serra was delighted to see a large number of rose bushes planted on each side of his doorway; they were covered with small delicate pink blossoms. His face glowed. "The Rose of Castile," he said. "Where did these precious gifts come from?"

"I brought them up with me from San Diego," Crespí answered.

Father Serra picked one of the small flowers. He inhaled the fragrance and a smile came to his weary face. "Praise God that I am allowed to work among such friends."

*   *   *

Father Serra spent the next year working in the mission at Carmel. The days found him in the fields, hoeing between rows of young corn plants side by side with the Indians. The corner of the hoe worked well when stubborn rocks needed to be pulled loose and the young Indian boys stacked the stones at the edge of the field to be used in future construction. Father Crespí was hitched behind the plow, breaking the ground where he intended to plant the orchard with a variety of Spanish pears.

The little priest also taught the Indian girls how to make garments out of the cloth that he had purchased in Mexico City. When he had sewn the last seam, he held a pair of pants in front of himself and all of the girls covered their mouths to hide their laughter. Father Serra looked at them and chuckled himself but all of them set to work with enthusiasm.

For over a year there had been no official word from Captain Rivera concerning the founding of Mission San Buenaventura, so Father Serra decided to travel the six miles to Monterey and see the captain himself. He stepped onto the porch and knocked on the door.

"Come in, it's open," Rivera shouted from his desk.

Father Serra walked in. "Good morning, Captain."

"What do you want?"

"There are some problems we need to resolve," the little priest said, not mincing words. "My first concern is the Mission San Buenaventura."

"I don't have the manpower, Padre. And besides, we're running out of supplies again with all of your new conversions."

"Viceroy Bucareli ordered the founding of this mission a long time ago. He has even marked it on his map because he believes that it exists."

"I will not discuss it. If I don't get some reinforcements, the mission will never be founded."

"Most of your men are idle and are causing trouble in the missions. If you put them to work in the fields, there would be no shortages."

Rivera grinned. "That's impossible. Most of my men joined the Army because they hate to farm. If I ordered that, they would abandon their posts."

"There's no need to be on half rations. The colonists' children are crying at night because they are going to bed hungry."

"You have all of the answers," Rivera said sarcastically. "Did you know that Mission San Juan Capistrano is to be founded?"

"No, I didn't."

"Lieutenant Ortega and Father Lasuén are preparing for that task this very minute. I'm worried because it will lessen the force in San Diego."

"There would be nothing to fear, Captain, if the molestations of the Indian women would cease. You see, I do know what transpires at the missions."

"I'll take care of my men, Padre. You have enough to do already."

"It's only the safety of the soldiers and the Indians that concerns me. If the Indians aren't treated any better, we're going to have trouble. I would like to avoid that if at all possible."

Rivera leaned across his desk. "At least we can agree on that."

Father Serra got up from the chair and limped toward the door. "I must prepare for a wedding to take place in the morning."

"By all means, Padre. That's a good job for you. Stop worrying about military matters."

Father Serra was frustrated and tired. "I've been told that before, many times," he paused at the door, "and it won't do you any good."

CHAPTER X

HE chapel at Carmel was small. It held only about one hundred and fifty people. It was filled to capacity and many people were standing against the walls to witness the marriage of Juan Evangelista and Terese. Father Serra faced the crowd with his book in hand. He had completed Mass and was now ready to begin the ceremony that would unite the couple in matrimony. Juan and Terese stood before Father Serra, waiting for the padre to begin. Juan was dressed in the fine clothes he had worn at the Viceroy's party: a blue jacket with gold buttons, white knickers, knee socks, and a pair of black leather shoes with large buckles.

Terese wore the white dress embroidered with roses and a delicate veil covered her face. Padre Serra read from the book, the two exchanged rings, and Juan faced his bride, lifted the veil, and kissed her softly on the lips. There was great joy on their faces as they walked down the center of the church. Father Serra held his place and looked on with pride, the same pride he could see on the faces of Juan's parents.

Father Serra went to his room after the great meal had been served to the guests. The courier had left his mail on his doorstep, so the padre picked it up and sat down at his desk to read it. The joy of the wedding day soon disappeared. Father Serra read the whole letter, then placed his glasses down on his desk and pushed the correspondence aside. Captain Rivera appeared at the door. He held a letter in his hand and he offered it to Father Serra. "Read this letter, Padre! The Mission San Diego has been attacked by Indians. Father Luís Jayme has been killed!"

"I have just received word of this unfortunate incident myself."

"Those savages will pay for it!" the officer snapped. "I promise you that!"

"California has its first martyr. Shouldn't we just let it go at that?"

"We're in trouble if the savages think that they can be successful against us."

"The Christian Faith teaches forgiveness, Captain. Reprisals will only leave them with hollow words and no choice but to war on us until they have driven us from their land."

"I will leave for San Diego immediately. You must remain behind."

"I ask you to reconsider, Captain. Even if I am their next victim, let them live long enough to save their souls."

"I will let you know how things progress," Rivera said as he walked into the compound and mounted his horse. He flicked the reins and eighteen soldiers followed him out of the mission gate in a cloud of dust.

Father Serra watched the troop ride away, then went into the chapel and prayed. For the next six months the padre tried to leave the Mission San Carlos to go to San Diego to help the priests there. He could not travel without an escort and Rivera had forbidden him to leave.

When letters came to him by courier, informing him that the captain was punishing even the innocent, it broke the old man's heart. After ten lashes, the victims would be cut down from the rafters of the porch and tossed outside the compound; then Rivera's soldiers would round up a new group to take their place. Finally, the little priest could stand it no longer, and went to see the officer Rivera had left in charge, Lieutenant Moraga.

"I have been hearing about Rivera's actions in San Diego and I must go there immediately."

"The Captain ordered me not to give you an escort."

"But he knows I must go. The missionaries there are so distraught they are talking about closing the mission and going back to Mexico."

"I hear that the Mission San Juan Capistrano has been abandoned because of the attack on Mission San Diego."

"Yes, it is true: one mission abandoned, the other left in ashes. It's a tragedy."

"I don't know what to tell you, Padre."

"There is another reason I must leave here," Father Serra said. "I have been given a *patente* that empowers me to confirm my many converts since there is no Bishop in upper California."

"I do have some good news for you, Padre."

"I could use a little of that," he said with a sigh.

"The Captain has ordered me to lead an expedition to San Francisco to build the Presidio there."

Father Serra was elated. "Praise God for that! If the fort is built, the missions will surely follow."

"I am supposed to lead all of the colonists. The *San Carlos* will carry most of our supplies."

"There must be room aboard for the mission bells, the farm implements, and the other items required to found two missions."

"I am sure we can find room, Padre. After all, most of us are your friends."

"With all of the Christian settlers going, there will be a need to send two missionaries."

"By all means, Padre. I was ordered only not to found a mission. The Captain said nothing about keeping Christian people from the Sacraments."

"I will send Fathers Palóu and Cambon. They are to found the next two missions."

"I will help them all that I can, Padre and still obey orders."

"I still need to go to San Diego."

"I think I've got it, Padre. There's only one way for you to get to San Diego without an escort, but don't tell the Captain that I told you of this."

"Would you care to tell me in confession?" Father Serra asked with a smile.

Moraga laughed. "Of course not, Padre. Now listen! The *San Antonio* will be leaving for San Diego soon. Captain Diego Choquet is also your friend and I am certain that Rivera didn't order him to deny you transport on his ship."

Father Serra breathed a sigh of relief. "I will be glad to be going where I am needed. I fear for the lives of those who are suffering."

"You look tired, Padre. You should rest."

"There's no time, my son. I must go where I am needed and wait for the Viceroy's reply regarding the reprisals that are being inflicted on the innocent."

"I am glad that the people in San Diego will be reunited with their father."

The padre shook the lieutenant's hand. "I must tell Father Palóu about this most fortunate turn of events and I must give praise to God for showing this most unworthy priest the way to do his work."

"God be with you, Father Serra."

* * *

During the next two weeks, the little priest helped Fathers Palóu and Cambon prepare for the trip to San Francisco and made arrangements for his own journey. When the land expedition headed north, Father Serra was on his way south. When the ship docked in San Diego, Captain Rivera came to meet with Captain Choquet. Rivera started up the gang plank as soon as it was set in place. "Permission to board," he called out to Choquet.

"Granted, Commandant. Besides, there's someone on board who wants to talk with you."

"Who is it?" Rivera asked, looking around.

The door to the captain's cabin swung open and Father Serra emerged. A look of fear appeared on Rivera's face.

"I have come to rebuild a mission and refound another," the little priest said as he started down the ramp.

Rivera looked as if he had seen a ghost. "Padre Serra!"

"Relax, Don Fernando. I haven't come to see the Viceroy, only to carry out his will."

Captain Rivera turned and darted away in panic, running into a sailor and knocking the man to the wooden dock. He kept running without looking back. "He's not only an idiot but he's a coward as well!" a sailor shouted as he helped his friend to his feet. The accusation was greeted with laughter from other sailors.

Within a short time, Father Serra and Captain Choquet were leading a work party to the burned mission. There was a crew of two dozen sailors and they carried a wide assortment of carpenter's tools, along with a selection of pistols and muskets. They all were anxious to get started with their work.

San Francisco de Asis

CHAPTER XI

APTAIN Rivera went to his quarters and immediately sought his bed. His confessor, Father Lasuén, sat in a chair by the captain's side.

"Now that the Father Presidente has come, the Viceroy will know all," Rivera said in a trembling voice. "And you know what happened to my predecessor!"

"Father Serra will speak only of your accomplishments. I know him well."

"I've never seen such determination in my life," Rivera said. "You just can't demoralize that little, crippled, old man. I should have known that he'd find a way to get out of Monterey."

"I assure you, Captain. The Padre will be too busy raising San Diego Mission from the ashes to bother you."

"I wouldn't be surprised if he went to see the Viceroy again," the captain mumbled. "And if there are no ships going south, he'll crawl all the way if he has to."

"He will rebuild the mission and, as Father Fuster has said, we may all be condemned to martyrdom."

Rivera only groaned and turned to face the wall.

The only thing that remained intact after the destruction of San Diego Mission was the stockade walls. Father Serra worked alongside Captain Choquet's crew. All of the men were covered with the soot they stirred up as they dismantled the charred remains in their preparations to rebuild.

Father Serra decided to replace the wooden buildings with adobe. Sailors were set to work making bricks, placing them, and plastering them. Two and half weeks later they were almost finished when Captain Rivera rode up onto the scene, accompanied by six heavily-armed soldiers who kept scanning the fields and hillside. Rivera inspected the area, seemingly surprised at the amount already done.

Father Serra and Captain Choquet, both working on the roof, soon noticed that he was there.

"I've got some bad news, Padre," Rivera yelled at them.

"What is it, Captain?" Serra asked, peering down at him.

"We have just received a report that there might be another uprising. You'll have to discontinue your work."

"Do you have any evidence?" Father Serra asked.

Captain Choquet climbed down the ladder. "If you are afraid of what the Indians might do to us, give us some more powder and shot and add three of your fine soldiers to our detail."

"I will not give away any powder and I need all of my soldiers for my own protection."

"Your plan of retreat, even before the attack, makes my men look like cowards."

Some of the sailors threw down their tools in disgust. There was grumbling among their ranks. "What are you afaid of, Captain?" one sailor asked. "You must have forty soldiers in the Presidio right now!"

"I'm glad I'm not in the Army," another sailor added. "I'd be embarrassed to death!"

Choquet raised his hand to quiet his men. "If you'd leave us alone, Captain, we'd soon have this work completed."

"I can't risk it," Rivera said. "I am responsible for your lives. And I am issuing an order. You will accompany me or I will arrest you and take you back in chains."

Choquet was forced to quiet his grumbling sailors again. For a moment it appeared that he might have a small mutiny on his hands. It was Father Serra who stepped between the two men.

"It is all right," he said, unable to keep the disappointment from his voice. "We will go. If we stay and the Indians come, more blood will flow. I will handle it in another way."

*   *   *

While waiting for the tides Captain Choquet kept his crew at the Presidio. After lying around for weeks, the men grew tired of their idleness. Relations between the soldiers and the contemptuous sailors became more strained. Finally, a courier rode into the compound and delivered some letters to Father Serra and Captain Rivera. The Viceroy had ordered the reprisals against the Indians stopped immediately. He also demanded that the mission work continue without any interference. An uncertain Captain Rivera rode north to San Francisco to assist Fathers Palóu and Cambon in their efforts there. Captain Choquet took his crew back to the Mission San Diego to complete the rebuilding there and Father Serra rode with Lieutenant Ortega to reestablish the mission at San Juan Capistrano. The priests had buried the mission bells when they abandoned the site earlier and now they dug them up and hung them from the beam that was still in place. Unafraid and with joy in his heart, the little priest rang the bells loudly. Soon many of the mission Indians returned with gifts of food.

"You will be safe here," the padre told the members of the expedition. "I have other work to do."

Serra was escorted north to Monterey by a contingent of six soldiers. As he rode into the compound of the Mission San Carlos, Father Crespí hurried to meet him. "You have an important visitor waiting, Padre," he said as he helped the weary man down from his saddle.

"Who is it, Juan?"

"Lieutenant Colonel Felipe Neve."

"Captain Rivera's replacement?"

"Yes. I will tell him that you have arrived while you dust yourself off," he said as he began to lead the donkey away.

"Thank you, Juan. I'll only be a minute."

Felipe Neve sat in a chair in the priest's quarters. As he tapped his fingers nervously on the edge of the desk, Father Serra came through the doorway. "I am sorry to have kept you waiting, Colonel, but your timing is right for I have just arrived. What may I do for you?"

"I came to tell you that I am to be the new Governor of upper California."

Father Serra nodded in approval and sat down at his desk. "The missions are beginning to produce well."

"And I will give you more livestock, fruit trees, seeds, and tools."

"Anything you can do will help our efforts."

"The immigrant families will not have their rations cut by me, as by my predecessor."

"They will be grateful to you and will serve you well, Governor."

"You should also prepare yourself for the founding of Mission San Buenaventura."

"The Viceroy has desired this for years."

"And I am here to carry out his orders."

"Praise God," he said. "I am ready to leave whenever I am asked."

"I also wanted to tell you that the Missions San Francisco and Santa Clara have been founded."

"We now have eight missions in upper California. The saints in heaven will be joyous."

"Don Fernando Rivera has been promoted to the rank of Lieutenant Colonel but he is now in Loreto. He will never bother you again."

Father Serra reflected for a moment. "He is the strongest and the healthiest man I have ever met."

Governor Neve rose from his chair. "I must not keep you from your work, Padre. If you need anything please let me know."

"God's children will be grateful to you for your generosity." Limping, the priest escorted him to the door and smiled wearily. "I, too, am overwhelmed. You are an answer to an old man's prayers." As they parted, Father Crespí appeared with a letter in his hand.

"This just arrived from our Guardian in San Fernando."

"I wonder what this could be about?"

"Do you suppose the Viceroy heard about your troubles with Captain Rivera?"

"Captain Choquet could have written him a letter."

"It must have been quite a letter, Padre."

"I have no control over what someone else writes."

"Maybe Lieutenant Ortega wrote a letter, too?" Crespí said, raising his eyebrows and grinning.

"Perhaps. Captain Choquet was exasperated after spending several months in San Diego," Father Serra said, "but I could never have accomplished as much as I did without his help and the help of his men."

"What did he think when you told him that restrictions had been placed on your authority as Father Presidente?"

"I never told him about it," the little priest said. "By the way, Captain Rivera is now a Lieutenant Colonel. May God bless him."

Serra put on his glasses, broke the letter's seal and read. "Wonderful news, Juan!"

"What is it?"

"Our Guardian has lifted the limitations that were imposed on me as Father Presidente. I can write to the Viceroy again but I pray that it won't be necessary."

"Did it go well with the Lieutenant Colonel?"

"Yes," he said. "Things seem to be settling down at last and just in time, for I will be making the rounds of the missions to use the confirmation powers that I have been given."

"The events in San Diego could have endangered the progress of all of the missions."

"It was by the grace of God that we went forward," Father Serra reminded him. "Fathers Lasuén and Paterna are at their posts and doing well."

"I believe that they no longer fear becoming martyrs. Father Serra? Padre! Are you all right?" Crespí rushed forward in alarm as the little priest began to cough so violently that his whole body shook. The attack was frightening and lasted for several minutes. Crespí ran for a pitcher of water and tried to comfort his friend as best he could. After a while, Father Serra regained his composure but his face was white and strained. He quivered and was forced to sit on his cot.

Crespí inspected him closely. "You must stay here and rest for a week or two, Padre. You are very ill, I fear."

"I have to use my confirmation powers before the *patente* runs out," Father Serra replied, drawing a deep shuddering breath. "I will rest tonight and, God willing, I will begin His duties tomorrow."

And so, an exhausted and obviously ailing Father Serra traveled from mission to mission. He always stopped briefly at Mission San Carlos but the word "rest" was not in his vocabulary. One night, as he read his correspondence, Father Crespí came in with a tray of food and set it down on a small table. "If you refuse to take care of yourself then it's up to me," he said. "I will force you to eat and, if you do not, I will write your friend, the Viceroy."

"Thank you, Juan," Father Serra said absent-mindedly and shook his head as he read a letter.

"Is something wrong, Padre?"

"The new Governor is violating the Law of the Indies. He is forcing the newly converted Indians to do slave labor in the Presidio in San Diego."

Father Crespí stiffened. "This is a serious matter."

"Father Lasuén also writes that the four Indians who killed Father Jayme have been arrested and condemned to death!"

"But the Viceroy has ordered no reprisals."

"I have instructed Father Lasuén to pray with them every day and to baptize them in prison if he has to."

"The sentence must be revoked!"

"This grieves me more than anything," Father Serra said with a tear in his eye. "I don't know how many times we have preached that the Christian faith is a faith of forgiveness."

"I can see why you often lose your appetite, Padre. I thought from the beginning that the new Governor was too good to be true."

"I know more than he wishes me to know," Father Serra said. "The *patente* to confirm gives me a chance to travel to each mission and witness all of his activities first-hand."

"You push yourself too hard, Padre. I wish you would slow down."

"I am fine, Juan. There is no reason for concern. Besides, there is . . . so much to be done . . . "

Father Crespí watched as the little priest's eyes closed and his head began to nod. Father Serra had not touched his food nor did he open his eyes when the tray was pushed aside.

Juan lifted his friend's legs onto the cot and eased him into a comfortable position before covering his frail body with a single blanket.

For a long time he stood there looking down at this man, this priest, this Father of the upper California missions. There was no doubt in Crespí's mind that Father Serra would die soon, a martyr to his beliefs, unless he curtailed his activities.

Father Juan made the sign of the cross and prayed, "God give him strength. Take the strength from me, if that be Thy will, but give him the energy to go about his work with faith and with his love of all your children."

Then he sat down to guard his sleeping friend.

⌒⚬∿⚬⌒

Santa Clara de Asis

CHAPTER XII

ATHER SERRA drove himself mercilessly, riding his donkey from mission to mission. His tour took several months since there were many converts to confirm and he was the only man in California who could administer the Sacrament. Early one morning Father Juan Crespí was working in one of the many gardens at the Mission San Carlos. He looked up from his work when he heard a donkey walk into the compound. He caught his breath when he saw Father Serra slowly slipping from the saddle. Running to his friend's side, he caught the little priest before he hit the ground.

As he tried to stand and regain his balance, Father Serra looked into Father Crespí's eyes. "Thank you, Juan. You're always right where I need you most."

"This is no time for jokes, Padre. Let me help you into your bed."

"What has transpired here while I was gone?"

"We'll have time for discussion later, Padre," he said, leading Father Serra to his quarters. "Relieve my heart. Get some rest."

Father Serra stopped. "There's something wrong, Juan, or you'd be wanting to talk from daylight to dark."

"After supper we will talk."

"Out with it, my friend."

Father Crespí paused for a moment. "All of California has lost a friend."

"Who, Juan?"

"The Viceroy Bucareli."

"He loved God's children as his own. May he be granted the eternal reward that he most certainly deserves."

Father Crespí began to cry. Tears streamed down his gentle face and he buried his head in his hands. Father Serra became very alert and now it was his turn to help Juan stay on his feet. "What is it, Juan? What else do you

63

have to tell me?"

Father Crespí was still crying. "I fear that this news will surely kill you, my friend."

"Tell me, Juan. I beg of you."

"I cannot find the words, my dear friend," he said. "Please, just follow me to the side of the church."

Father Serra sighed, then hurried behind Father Crespí down a long, flower-lined path. They finally stopped in front of a double headstone that marked a pair of fresh graves. A Rose of Castile was growing in front of the marker. Father Serra read the inscription:

EVANGELISTA

JUAN   TERESE

AUG. 19   AUG. 12

1778

Father Serra dropped to his knees beside the graves and he clasped his hands together in agony. "Oh, my dear, sweet friends."

"I was with them until the end, Padre."

"Juan was such a great ambassador for his people and I trust that he fills that capacity again!"

"They had no children of their own."

"They were but children themselves," he said, "beautiful children of God."

Father Crespí continued to cry. "I tried to help them, Padre," he said with outstretched hands, "but their fevers were so high."

Father Serra rose to his feet with tears in his eyes. "I trust that you will care for their rose before you even consider looking after mine?"

"If that is your wish, my friend, it will be done."

Father Serra was visibly shaken. Father Crespí put his arm around the old man and they walked toward Father Serra's quarters very slowly. "My confirmation powers have been curtailed by Governor Neve," Father Serra said.

"Now you will at last get some rest and relieve my heart."

Father Crespí helped Father Serra to his bed. Juan did everything he could to nurse the old man back to health but nothing seemed to work. Father Serra's legs were infected and swollen again and he could hardly breathe as a result of his asthmatic condition.

The best medicine for Father Serra came with the opportunity to sing with the mission children. He had the voice of an angel and, when it was time for choir practice, it was impossible to keep the little priest in bed. Over the next few months, the padre taught the Indian children of Carmel how to sing the beautiful Gregorian chants. The choir performed splendidly under his guidance because he had the patience to help the children attain perfection. He never grew tired of practicing and neither did the children because he made it fun.

The next year of Father Serra's life was one of his happiest; he remained in Carmel for the entire year awaiting the reinstatement of his confirmation powers. As he practiced singing with the children one day, a visitor came to see him. Father Crespí went to tell Father Serra and he gestured with his hand because he didn't want to interrupt in the middle of a chorus. When the children concluded, Father Serra turned to Father Crespí. "What is it, Juan?"

"Governor Neve is here to see you, Padre."

"Where is he?"

"In the flower garden," Father Crespí said as he pointed.

"Take over, Juan. I will be right back."

Father Crespí had a sheepish look on his face as Father Serra walked away. The children started to sing again and Father Crespí joined in with his bullfrog voice. Most of the children blushed and covered their mouths with their hands as they laughed. Serra looked back before he rounded the corner and smiled at his friend's unusual vocal quality.

Governor Neve was sitting on a rough-hewn log that served as a bench. He looked up when he heard the priest coming toward him. "Have you heard the news, Padre?" he asked. "The city of Los Angeles has been founded. I have signed the charter!"

Father Serra paused in thought. "This is a bad policy, founding cities without missions and without padres to keep order."

"What makes you so sure?"

"I have also heard that Don Fernando Rivera is dead!"

Neve's cockiness disappeared. "Oh?"

"Yes, Governor. That is the end result of this experiment," he said. "The Lieutenant Colonel dead, all of his men, and the colonists, including their wives and children. Dead!" Father Serra pounded his fist into his hand. "And so are our chances of bringing the Indians of Yuma into the family of God for at least fifty years!"

"Who told you this?"

"Does it matter, Governor? The damage has been done. Perhaps God will be kinder to you than history."

"It will be different in Los Angeles!"

"Your plan to have the colonists teach the Indians isn't feasible," the padre said. "For how can one teach what he does not already know?"

Neve glared at Serra. "The Dominicans will probably come to upper California and displace your Order as they did in lower California!"

"I have heard this rumor also. And I know if they come it is by the will of God," Father Serra answered with confidence. "Therefore, I will do all I can to assist them so my children do not suffer in the transition."

"I must go and make sure that my experiment goes well."

"I will pray for everyone who lives there."

Governor Neve stood and walked down the path. Father Serra went after him. The children were still singing. "Do you hear that, Governor?"

"What, Padre?"

"The voices of angels," the little priest said. "Please come with me for a moment."

"I don't have the time. I must go to Los Angeles and see that all goes well."

"Don't you care to see those you are responsible for?"

"All right," he said reluctantly, "but only for a minute."

Father Serra walked slowly around the corner, with Neve following. "Listen!"

The priest and the governor stood where the children could not see them. Father Crespí had stopped singing; he directed only with hand signals.

Serra turned to the governor. "This is the purpose of the mission effort: bringing people closer to God and teaching them to work together in harmony," he said. "Can those who do not know this accomplish so much? Is there security when the blind lead the blind?"

Governor Neve glared at Father Serra and walked angrily away.

"I hope you come visit again, when Father Crespí and I come back from the northern mission," the padre called after the departing figure, then blessed him with the sign of the cross.

Neither Father Serra nor Father Crespí were physically well when they began their arduous tour of the two northern missions. Father Serra wanted to confirm the converts because he feared that his health might make the trip impossible in the future. When the small expedition, escorted by six soldiers, rode through the gate at Mission San Francisco, they were met by Father Francisco de Palóu.

"I have been awaiting your arrival, Padres!" he said joyfully.

Father Serra looked around at the buildings and the gardens. "Things are certainly going well for you here."

"Lieutenant Moraga is still very enthusiastic, Padre."

Father Juan Crespí smiled. "Father Palóu?" he said.

"Yes, Juan?"

"Will you kindly help me down from this beast?"

"Yes, certainly," Father Palóu responded.

"This animal has either grown a foot taller on our journey or my legs have become a foot shorter!"

Serra laughed. "You're still a young man, Juan."

"That's what I tell myself every time I look at you, Padre, but I just can't keep up with you any longer," he said grinning. "You win!"

All three priests laughed heartily as Palóu helped Father Crespí down from the mule.

Palóu turned to Father Serra. "You were in need of rest the last time I saw you," he said, "and you obviously need it now. Don't you ever slow down, even for a week or so?"

Father Crespí interrupted. "Are you kidding? He's still the same!"

"In that case I will tell you that there are many confirmations to perform before you leave, Junípero, but I hope that you will rest first."

"Schedule them for the morning, Francisco," Father Serra said.

"But there are nearly seventy, Padre!"

Father Serra smiled. "Why, that's wonderful, Francisco!"

Father Crespí began to cough. He wheezed asthmatically, as Father Serra had done earlier. Palóu watched him, concerned. "Are you sure you should have made this journey?"

"Don't worry about it, Padre. I always cough like this when I get this far north. It must be the dampness," he said. "I will be happy to go with Padre Serra to found Mission San Buenaventura in the south!"

By the time the confirmations had been completed at Missions San Francisco and Santa Clara, Crespí's health had grown much worse and the weather had deteriorated. A limping Padre Serra had to lead the priest's mule most of the way back to Mission San Carlos. Crespí soon slumped over in his saddle but Father Serra pressed onward, despite the wind and driving rain.

Once home again, Crespí was assisted to his quarters where Serra cared for him. After they had prayed together, the little priest left to allow Juan to rest. When Father Serra returned a short time later, he found his friend asleep in the Lord. His crucifix was clutched to his breast and he was staring at the ceiling. Father Serra wept as he said a prayer, then he closed the eyes of his companion for the final time.

Many people stood outside awaiting word of Juan's condition. Father Serra's expression told them the news. The Indians began to lament as Father Serra walked to the beam and tolled the bells.

That evening in his quarters he wrote in the mission records that Father Juan Crespí had died on January 1, 1782, and was to be buried at the Mission San Carlos in Carmel. It was the beginning of a new year. Perhaps the little priest sensed he would not see another one. He went outside and stared at the row after row of fruit trees in Juan Crespí's orchard. A cold wind blew the scudding clouds across the face of the moon. The trees were bare, devoid of leaves and fruit. To the untrained eye they looked dead and yet Serra knew that within a few weeks they would be ablaze with color and new life and, by mid-summer, they would be heavy with God's fruit for His children.

The orchard was a legacy from Juan Crespí, a legacy that stretched across two hundred years of time, for today, three of the original trees are still bearing fruit!

❧

San Buenaventura

CHAPTER XIII

N February of 1782 Father Serra was informed by letter that Governor Neve wanted the mission San Buenaventura founded. Rather than answer the correspondence, Father Serra went directly to the site. Lieutenant José Ortega led the land expedition, with Father Cambon accompanying the group. Father Serra had been given permission to confirm his converts and he continued to fulfill that responsibility as well, in spite of his failing health.

By the time California's ninth mission had been founded, Father Serra was in desperate physical condition. He was over sixty-eight years old when he rode into the compound at Mission San Carlos and was met by his new assistant, Father Noriega.

Nearly unconscious, Father Serra had to be carried to his quarters. His face was covered with dust that had adhered to his fevered skin. Father Noriega poured some water into a large bowl and attempted to clean Father Serra's hands and face with a damp cloth. When he removed the old man's sandals, he saw that the straps had cut deeply into the flesh. Father Serra stirred. "Lie still, Padre," Father Noriega implored. "This time you must get some rest."

Father Serra held onto his colleague's arm. "Only for a day or two, then I must visit all of the missions for the third and last time."

"The last time, Padre?"

"My confirmation powers run out in less than a year," he explained wearily. "When the Governor curtailed them I confirmed anyway because I was afraid that I wouldn't make it back. But this is different. The Holy Father in Rome gave me only ten years to attend to this responsibility." Anything else he might have said was cut off as his weakened body was racked with a coughing attack. It was a long time before he could breathe normally again.

"Please, Padre. You must slow down for a while."

"I will sail to San Diego, then I will work my way back north."

"You can sail south with no trouble but the winds have been unfavorable and you will probably have to come back by land."

"I received a letter from our Guardian in San Fernando," Serra said, wheezing again in his effort to talk. "I have been instructed to found no more missions until the Spanish government changes its methods."

"Could it mean a change of governors?"

"I have seen many men come and go."

Father Noriega rung out the cloth and wiped Father Serra's face once more. "Sleep now, Padre."

"Only for a little while," was his reply. "I must not miss my ship."

Father Noriega left the room and gently closed the door. When he returned at midnight, he saw the little priest on his knees praying.

Father Serra sailed to San Diego before the week was out. He stood at the rail and squinted in the bright sunlight. His hair was now snow white, his face was tanned dark brown and etched with wrinkles but his eyes still contained their youthful enthusiasm. The first thing he did on arriving in San Diego was to visit the old cemetery. He walked down a long row of grave markers that contained dates that ranged from June, 1769 to March 15, 1770, carrying a small bunch of wildflowers. He stopped and placed them on the grave of his young Indian friend, José Maria Vergerano, the youth who had died when an arrow pierced his neck on August 15, 1769.

Father Serra knelt on the ground and made the sign of the cross. His eyes glistened and tears streamed down his cheeks. He heard the footsteps of approaching people and turned to see them. Father Lasuén stood close by, with four Indian men at his side. They were clad in the white pajama-like costume that designated that they were Christians. Father Serra made the sign of the cross and rose awkwardly to his feet. Father Lasuén gasped when he saw how poor the Father Presidente's health was.

"Padre!" Lasuén called out.

Serra wiped his eyes with the cloth he carried in his sleeve. "That is the grave of the young boy who died in my arms so many years ago." He paused and sighed. "What can I do for you?"

"These four men have asked to see you before you leave us," Lasuén replied. "And I thought now would be the best time, before you are exhausted from performing so many confirmations during the next several days."

"Yes. Do I know them?"

"No, but there is something they must say to you."

"By all means," Father Serra said as he faced a man who had stepped out of the group as spokesman. The man dropped to his knees and began to cry. "We are the four men who took the life of Father Luís Jayme and we have come to thank you for pleading for our lives."

"Rise to your feet, my son. The Lord God has forgiven you."

The man did as instructed. "We wanted you to know of our repentance, Padre."

Father Serra extended his hands and a smile came across his face. "Oh, praise God that all of you have lived long enough to save your souls!" he said and turned to Father Lasuén. "This is another indication of the excellent work you have done here in San Diego, Padre. I will write to our Guardian and tell him so."

Lasuén smiled. "You may take my mule when you go north again."

"Thank you but I must walk all the way to San Francisco."

Father Lasuén didn't question the padre's motivation. The young priest knew that Father Serra was too ill to ride and he also knew that the little priest would never mention his failing health.

Father Serra blessed each of the four men who had come to see him, then turned and limped away. The padre finished his work at San Diego and set out alone for his first stop at Mission San Juan Capistrano.

From Capistrano, he visited San Gabriel Mission and ignored their pleas that he remain until his swollen leg healed. He stopped at San Buenaventura only long enough to confirm his converts and then continued up the coast until he reached the cliffs of Santa Barbara. He had come to a dead end, further travel by shore was impossible. The padre prepared to retrace his steps when he was noticed by several unconverted Indians hunting at the top of the bluff. Seeing his predicament, they came to his aid. In gratitude, the padre touched each of them on the forehead, blessing them. Soon they hoisted him up onto their shoulders and carried him up a steep path. At the top of the path the Indians set him down carefully and then walked at his side. When they had traveled several miles together, a new group of Indians took their place and continued north with the priest, giving him protection, food, and companionship.

When Father Serra finally reached the Mission San Carlos, he saw a fine horse tied up to the hitching post in front of his quarters. Astonished, he saw Pedro Fages sitting near his door. Fages rose to his feet and approached the little priest. "I was informed by a young Indian boy that you were at Mission San Antonio last night, Padre, so I came to wait for you here."

"It is good that you came," Father Serra said. "I will not be here very long for I must go to the northern missions."

"I want you to know that I wish to provide, for the missions, the mail service that my predecessor discontinued."

"So, you are the new Governor of California?"

"Yes, Padre," he said. "And an older and wiser man I assure you."

"I will continue to pray for you," the padre said, "as always."

Fages helped the crippled priest to his room and shook his head in wonder. "You haven't changed a bit," he said. "You work yourself into exhaustion. I'd better leave now and let you get some rest."

"In two or three days I set out for the northern missions."

"God go with you, Padre."

"May He help both of us to make wise decisions."

Serra started out for the northern missions three days later. As he walked he saw the Indian villages along the winding trail. The faces of these people were dirty, their living conditions deplorable, and the sight brought him to tears. He reached Mission San Francisco by late afternoon. Father Palóu was surprised to see him. "Junípero, I didn't expect to see you again!"

The little priest's voice was weak when he replied, "My power to confirm will run out soon and there's a new church to dedicate at Mission Santa Clara."

"We can talk about work after you have rested."

"I need to confess my sins," Serra said.

"What would you like first, Padre, sleep or confession?"

"I am so concerned about the possible Dominican take over," he said. "It must be the result of my sins."

Father Palóu smiled and shook his head in disbelief. "You keep talking about your sins, my dear friend, but you have never sinned in your life."

"It's what I haven't done that concerns me most. I have walked the trails between all the missions many times and I have counted twenty-one Indian villages within view of the paths."

"But you were limited to how many converts you could baptize, Padre. How could they all be fed?"

"If that thought makes you feel better, Francisco, then so be it. But they could be fed and hopefully before any of them die unbaptized and are denied membership into the family of God."

"Do you wish to pray before confession, Padre?"

"I am ready, Francisco. Our talk has helped me to organize my thoughts."

Father Serra knelt on the hard, tile floor and made the sign of the cross. Father Palóu knelt before him and began a prayer in Latin.

When the little priest returned to the Mission San Carlos, he was followed by a crowd of people. They were singing as they walked when Father Serra raised his hand for them to stop. He saw an unbaptized Indian child playing with a crude homemade crucifix. It had been tied together with a leather thong. Father Serra blessed the child while the rest of the people in the village looked on. Father Serra continued on his way with a heavy heart because he wanted so much to be able to work with the Indians he had just left behind. It was as if he knew his strength was fading, not to be renewed this time.

The little old man was coughing terribly by the time he reached his home at the Mission San Carlos. Father Noriega knew that Serra was very ill, so he dispatched a letter by courier to San Francisco:

Dear Father Palóu,

You must come quickly to the Mission San Carlos. The Father Presidente is dying!

Fr. Noriega

Palóu left as soon as he received the note. He rode to Mission San Carlos as quickly as he could travel. As he approached, the voices of children could be heard and soon he identified the voice of Father Serra leading the choir in song. Father Palóu approached an old mission guard and said, "The Father Presidente seems in fine health today!"

The old soldier shook his head. "Do not deceive yourself, Padre. He's always in fine voice when he prays or sings but take my word for it," he said sadly, "it's hopeless."

Despondent, Palóu went to Father Serra's quarters to wait. He sat down at his friend's desk and examined the worn, wire-rimmed spectacles and the quill that had been used to write so much important correspondence. Finally he heard Father Serra coughing as he neared his quarters.

"Francisco," the little priest said, "thank God you have come!"

"Father Noriega sent for me."

"I have always prayed that you would be with me at the end."

"We have known each other for thirty-five years, Padre."

"Has it been that long, Francisco?"

"Yes," he said, his voice husky with emotion.

"There is still so much to do."

There was a knock on the door and Father Palóu opened it as Father Serra began to cough again. A man entered the room with a black bag in his hand. "I am Juan Garcia," he said. "I am a ship's doctor. My Captain sent me ahead when he heard that you were ill, Padre."

"Is the captain on his way?"

"Yes, Captain Canizares is very concerned about you."

"Can you do something for this man?" Father Palóu pleaded.

"He is coughing so violently," the doctor said. "If I cauterize his flesh it may loosen the phlegm."

Father Serra's breathing was labored when he responded. "I have refused to be treated by doctors all of these years, choosing instead to be reliant on the Divine Physician. But perhaps He does not wish me to get better this time, so do whatever you wish."

The doctor went to the mission kitchen and returned with a cast-iron pot full of coals. He placed several irons into the pot and waited for them to glow white hot. Using a pair of tongs, the doctor picked up a piece of the hot metal. Father Serra lay on his bed with his chest bare, waiting for the doctor's remedy. Father Palóu turned his head as the hot iron sizzled on the little priest's flesh. The old man remained motionless; not even a blink of an eye indicated the agony he must have been experiencing.

Finally the doctor removed the iron and dropped it into the charcoal pot.

"Are you finished with your work?" Father Serra asked calmly.

"Yes," the man said.

While Garcia collected his tools, Father Serra sat up in his bed and began to cut out clothing for the Indian children who lived at the mission. The physician walked away. "Someone else can do that," Father Palóu said.

The old man smiled. "No, Francisco. Doing for God's children is the work that I enjoy!"

The next morning, after Mass, Father Palóu peeked his head through Serra's door.

The padre rested on his bed and he turned his head toward his friend. "Did you save a consecrated host for me?" he asked.

"Yes, as you requested."

"I wish to receive the Sacrament in church."

"But, Padre. I can bring the Sacrament to you."

"He need not come to me when I can go to Him."

Father Serra sat up in bed and laboriously rose to his feet. He limped slowly toward the door. A large crowd of soldiers and Indians gathered outside his quarters. Many of them had tears in their eyes. They followed Father Serra to church at a snail's pace. He paused before a table that had been made ready for the occasion. Raising his hand in the air, Father Serra began to lead them in song with his usual strong voice. Some of the people attempted to join in but their voices were choked with emotion. When the song was concluded, Father Palóu gave communion to his dying friend.

Father Serra emerged from the church and a long procession of weeping people followed: soldiers, muleteers, Christian and non-Christian Indians, colonists, and sailors. Father Palóu stationed himself outside Serra's door. Others in attendance heard the frail, old man coughing during the long night. Father Serra never slept and the people burned candles all night long while they prayed. The youngest children slept on blankets on the ground at their mothers' feet. When the sun peeked over the hill, the people extinguished their candles. Father Serra hadn't coughed for some time and all of the people were very anxious. As Father Palóu opened the door to Father Serra's quarters, the contingent became silent, then cheered as Father Serra emerged from the door looking strong again.

"You have visitors, Padre," Father Palóu said.

"Who has come, Francisco?"

"Captains Canizares and Diaz."

"Ring the bells for them," Serra said. "They are honored guests!"

Fathers Serra and Palóu met the two men in the mission dining room. They embraced each other and sat down at a large table as the bells began to ring.

Father Serra turned to Captain Canizares. "I remember when you refused to abandon me in San Diego."

The man smiled. "When you said that you'd stay and eat the grass I believed you, Padre."

"And then you helped me escape from San Diego, when Pedro Fages ordered me not to leave the country."

Canizares laughed. "Life does take strange turns, Padre, but one thing is certain. It is always a pleasure to have you on board my ship."

Captain Diaz spoke up. "After all, Padre, who could take better care of his crew when they're seasick?"

Everyone laughed heartily.

"I have heard that you have just returned from Peru," Father Serra said to Canizares.

"Yes, Padre. Most of the country down there is high up in the mountains."

Father Serra smiled. "God must hear their prayers first."

There was a round of laughter, then everyone fell silent. "I want to thank you for traveling so far just to throw a little earth on my grave," Padre Serra said.

"But this cannot be, Padre," Canizares said. "We believe that you will be better soon."

Captain Diaz sat up in his chair. "And that you will once again be founding missions."

"This kindness is an act of mercy for which I shall be forever grateful," the little priest said as he turned to Palóu. "Bury me in the church, beside Father Juan Crespí. When the stone church is built, let them put me where they wish."

Father Palóu wiped his eyes. "If it is God's will, we will comply."

Father Serra nodded his head slowly.

"I beseech you, Padre," Palóu began, "when you draw near the presence of the Holy Trinity, offer adoration on my behalf. And after that, never forget me."

Serra nodded his head. Palóu continued. "Also remember these missions that you are leaving orphaned and the people here with you now."

"I promise you that if God grants me the eternal reward, which I don't deserve, I will pray for each and every one of you and also for all of those who are still unconverted."

Father Serra stood up, smiled wearily at them, and limped back to his quarters. The crowd was still standing silently near his door. He blessed them before stepping into the room. Fathers Palóu and Noriega and Captains Canizares and Diaz followed the old man into his quarters. Before the door was closed, Dr. Garcia, some sailors, and several Christian Indians had crowded in as well.

"Sprinkle my room with holy water!" Father Serra commanded.

"Do you feel an uneasiness?" Palóu asked.

"No, but this will forestall it."

Father Serra sat quietly for a couple of minutes while the others began to pray. "I am afraid! I am afraid!" he suddenly cried out.

"I am here, Padre," Palóu responded.

"I am in terror! Recite the prayer for the dying, and loudly, so I can hear!"

Father Palóu recited the prayer that commended the soul of the dying to God. Father Serra sat in his chair and responded when the prayer had been concluded. "God be praised! All of my fears have vanished!"

Serra was silent for a few moments, then drew a deep breath and said, "Goodbye, my friends, please leave me now with Father Palóu."

One by one, weeping, they filed out of the room. Father Serra quietly read his office from a prayer book as Palóu watched. When the old man had concluded, he placed his glasses on his desk for the final time. Father Palóu gave him a small cup of hot broth.

Father Serra took a sip, then handed it back to his friend. "Thank you, Francisco. Let me now go to rest."

Father Serra went to his bed. He held his crucifix to his chest with both hands. Palóu turned and silently left the room.

At just a few minutes before two o'clock Saturday afternoon, August 28, 1784, Father Junípero Serra went to his heavenly reward. The bells at the Mission San Carlos began to toll.

CHAPTER XIV

ATHER Francisco Palóu made all of the arrangements for the funeral. He dressed his teacher and friend in a fresh robe of the Franciscan Order. Father Serra was placed on a bier and laid before the altar in the chapel. Soldiers blocked the entrance while the preparations were being made, their lances crossed to block the way. Governor Pedro Fages stood in front of the door with Lieutenant Morago on one side and Lieutenant José Francisco Ortega on the other. The small mission compound was filled with thousands of people. From the governor's vantage point he could see people walking toward the chapel in a never-ending flow from the hills surrounding the mission: soldiers of every rank, sailors, ships' captains, colonists, Christian and non-Christian Indians and their chiefs. As they entered the mission compound, each was given a single flower to be given as a parting gift to their Father and friend.

Inside the church, Fathers Palóu and Noriega finished their preparations. Father Serra rested in a simple redwood casket. He was dressed in a gray robe with a new white cord tied around his waist. A metal crucifix rested on his chest in his folded hands. His hair was snow white and his face was still slightly brown from the weathering it had taken.

The Indian children, who made up the choir, were dressed in powder-blue pajama-like costumes. They were all in their places, waiting for Father Noriega to lead them in song. Father Palóu let himself out through the side entrance and informed the governor that all was ready.

Pedro Fages stepped forward with raised hands and the crowd fell silent immediately, although most of them were still in tears. The mission bells stopped their dirge.

The governor spoke, "We have all assembled here today to pay our last respects to a man who has influenced our lives," he began. "But how many of us realize that this gentle servant of God has influenced the history of this great and abundant land forever? Without his love, dedication, and undying faith in God, this land would still be nothing but an untamed wilderness." Fages paused to clear his throat and to wipe the tears from his eyes. "A long time ago, before I realized the things I am telling you today, I called this man 'a lover of flowers' and a 'lover of children.' I said that in contempt, in the heat of anger. But now I repeat the statement because I am moved by his love. Long after all of us have been forgotten and our tombstones have turned into dust, millions of people will come from the ends of the earth to stand by his grave and pay homage to Father Junípero Serra."

The bells began to peal again. The doors to the chapel were swung open and the people entered in a single file. The choir began to sing the Gregorian chants and their voices echoed out of the small room like the boom of a cannon. One by one they filed past the body of Father Junípero Serra. Each made the sign of the cross as they passed and each dropped a single Rose of Castile on the bier and left through the side door. In a very short time, the body of the little priest seemed to be floating on an ocean of pink roses. They were piled high and they spilled over the communion rail and out onto the main floor.

About the Author

Mark Brunelle was born in Oregon City, Oregon in 1949. He grew up in that state where he worked as a journeyman cement mason, a construction worker, and in the forests that cover the Warm Springs Indian Reservation in Central Oregon.

The author moved to the Monterey Peninsula with his wife and two children in June 1980 and immediately became interested in the life and work of Father Junipero Serra after a visit to the Mission San Carlos in Carmel.

Since he has lived in California, Mark has written extensively, completed his college education, and become very knowledgeable in early California history.